W9-BMT-103

40 Rubrics & Checklists

TO ASSESS READING AND WRITING

BY ADELE FIDERER

SCHOLASTIC
PROFESSIONAL BOOKS

NEW YORK • TORONTO • LONDON • AUCKLAND • SYDNEY
MEXICO CITY • NEW DELHI • HONG KONG

Acknowledgements

*I*n most states today the development of literacy standards has become a hot topic as well as a reality. Consequently, the idea for this book grew out of teachers' requests for practical tools that would help them develop criteria for assessing—and improving—their students' reading and writing abilities through authentic classroom activities. And so I dedicate this book to all these teachers, who are working so hard to improve literacy.

I would like to thank the following teachers for their contributions to the book's reading, writing, and project assessments:

Maddy Stempel for her students' character analyses, writings, and science dioramas. I am also grateful to Maddy and Margery Manber for sharing materials they used to meet their new statewide standards for English Language Arts.

Mary Alice Hratko for her students' letter-writing assessments as well as her personal evaluation of this book's letter-writing project and materials

Frances Seaman and Carol DeMay for their independent reading rubric

The many teachers in the Scarsdale Public Schools whose students' writing samples enrich this book

My longtime friends, Leda Canino and Lila Fagenson, who used their teaching expertise to help me score and annotate the student writing samples that appear in Writing Exemplars Grades 3–6

My editor, Suzanne Stroble, who offered excellent suggestions—as well as rubrics—for this book. Suzanne's knowlege of rubric assessment, grounded in current research, grew out of her own teaching experiences with sixth graders.

The reproducibles may be photocopied for classroom use only. No other part of this publication may be reproduced in whole or in part, stored in a retrieval system in any form by any means, electronic or mechanical, photocopying, recording, or otherwise, without written permission of the publisher. For information regarding permission, write to Scholastic Inc., 555 Broadway, New York, NY 10012.

Front cover and interior design by Kathy Massaro

ISBN # 0-590-01787-X
Copyright © 1999 by Adele Fiderer.
All rights reserved.
Printed in the U.S.A.

Contents

Introduction

What is the place of rubrics in your assessment program? Take a moment to consider all the different ways you gather information to evaluate each student's literacy development over time. Perhaps you create book "quizzes" to determine how many important facts a student can correctly recall about a story. You probably rely on formal evaluations such as placement tests, standardized tests, and unit tests to determine how well each student performs in relation to the larger group. And, if you are like me and most teachers I know, you also ask your students to respond to the texts they read for their literature- and content-area studies in a variety of creative ways—for example, by constructing a project, by giving a presentation, or by writing an essay such as those on page 5.

Although we may have a general idea in our heads of which of these work products is "excellent," "good," "satisfactory," or "poor," a more precise and thorough way of explaining our ratings would help us guide all our students to improve their performances.

As most of us who teach have already discovered, assessment requires a balanced information-gathering process to provide a clear picture of each student as a reader and writer. We use surveys to determine our students' reading and writing preferences, writing portfolios to discover evidence of writing development over time, and more formal evaluations such as placement tests, standardized tests, and unit tests to determine the mastery of a specific skill and to show where each student performs in relation to the larger group. Now rubrics—the newest arrivals on the assessment scene—allow us to interpret and evaluate a greater variety of rich and complex work products and performances than ever before: a report on Abraham Lincoln, an analysis of a story character, a personal essay, a model of a rain forest, or even a letter to Pizza Hut complaining about a soggy crust.

Diving Beetle

Down it dives with with a bubble captured under its wing. What is it? A Diving Beetle of course, named for the way it moves through the water. A baby Diving Beetle is called a larva. Some people call them Water Tigers because of their terrible habits. They will just grab any insect, even insects larger then themselves. The beetle breaks open its jaws and swallows.

When the larva grows a little it makes itself a little kind of a crib underground with a hard bottom. It goes into its crib upsidedown. After a few months, it comes out with a hard shell from the bottom of the crib. It is a grownup now and can dive down through the water.

The Diving Beetle eats (cont) algae and other pond plants. If you go to a pond or a stream you will probably find it in the algae or duckweed.

▲

How would you rate these reports? Look at the rubrics on pages 99 and 100 for scoring tips.

What are fossils?

If you don't know what fossils are, you should read this. Well" I guess you decided to read this! O.K. lets get going! Um, how about you "asking me a question first! O.K. "What are fossils, it is. You think your so smart, well hows this? Fossils are inprints or casts of bones of animals, trees, bugs or dinosaurs. If you think thats good, listen to this: Fossils are made by either: a dinosaur steps into mud the mud dries 2 hundred million years pass, a palentologest finds it, its a fossil! or lets say a fish died millions of years a go. It fell in the mud. The mud burried it and the skin and muskles disinagrate, then miner-alls from earth and rain. The minecalls turn the bones into stone.

USING RUBRICS FOR PERFORMANCE ASSESSMENTS

What we are after, then, is a tool that describes the knowledge and skills a particular project or performance demonstrates, based on specific criteria for quality work. Because they provide such explanations, rubrics enable us to interpret and even assign a score to complex student work. If you've glanced at any of the rubrics in this book, you have noticed that rubrics are scales that display three or more levels of achievement. Each level provides a numerical score and/or a label that defines a different degree of mastery or success. To determine a score, you would need to carefully examine or observe a student's performance or work product, keeping in mind the criteria for a successful performance. Then you would match your impressions of the performance to the rubric level that best describes it.

AN EXAMPLE OF RUBRIC SCORING

The following rubric was designed by a teacher to assess her students' research project presentations.

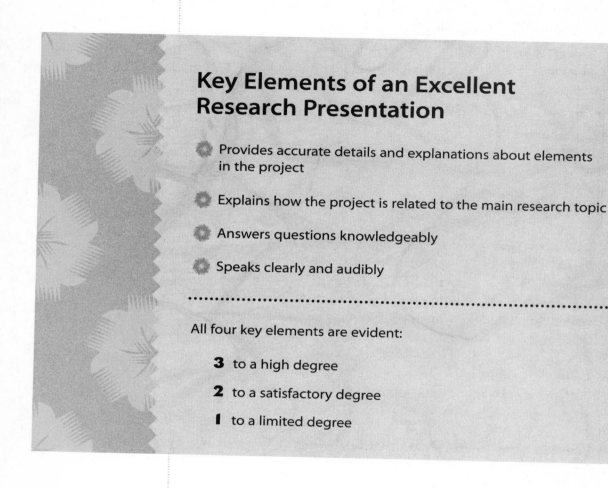

Key Elements of an Excellent Research Presentation

⚙ Provides accurate details and explanations about elements in the project

⚙ Explains how the project is related to the main research topic

⚙ Answers questions knowledgeably

⚙ Speaks clearly and audibly

All four key elements are evident:

3 to a high degree

2 to a satisfactory degree

1 to a limited degree

KEY BENEFITS OF RUBRIC ASSESSMENT

⚙ You can adapt or create a rubric to fit a wide variety of reading and writing activities in your curriculum.

⚙ If your school district has developed literacy standards for each grade level, you can use rubrics to determine how well your students are meeting those standards.

⚙ You'll find that rubrics can inform and improve your teaching. The criteria you use to determine a high-level or excellent performance provide directions for your teaching and goals for your students.

- Once your students have a clear understanding of the particular skills you will be looking for in a project or performance, they are more likely to produce better work.

- Rubrics can be time savers. With some practice, you should be able to make an assessment in just a few minutes after reading or examining a student's work product.

Questions Teachers Ask

HOW DO I USE THE RUBRICS IN THIS BOOK?

Start by looking at the TABLE OF CONTENTS for a section that matches a language arts-related activity going on in your classroom right now. For example, if your students are analyzing characters in a novel, writing essays or research papers, or creating science projects this book's TABLE OF CONTENTS will help you locate an appropriate rubric for assessing their work.

After selecting a rubric, review its criteria for an excellent performance. The criteria will give you a clear idea of what you will be looking for in your students' work. Of course, you may want to modify the criteria to fit your own specific needs. You will also find blank forms for creating your own rubrics on pages 121–127 of this book. Once you become accustomed to them, you will be delighted with the ease of rubric assessment.

HOW DO I USE A RUBRIC TO SCORE MY STUDENTS' WORK?

With practice, you'll find that scoring is a quick and reliable task, but there are some things you should know about the process. Following are tips for scoring which you may want to photocopy for easy reference.

Tips for Scoring

- When reading a student's response or examining a project, refer to the rubric frequently. Ask yourself which descriptions best match the student's work, but keep in mind that there is some variation within each level. For example, some papers or work products might be a high 3, others a middle 3, and some a low 3. For this reason, you may wish to use pluses or minuses to make finer distinctions.

- Be sure to focus only on the criteria in the rubric and avoid comparing students' papers. When in doubt, refer to the student's prewriting organizer. Some students may write more on an organizer than on a blank sheet because it is a more directed task. Thus the organizer as well as the final product can provide evidence that the student has mastered a particular skill.

- Record the score or developmental level on the CLASS RECORD FORM on page 128. It's a good idea to store the work products that you have assessed in individual folders or containers so that you can readily refer to them at a future time—when writing report cards, for example, or to prepare for a conference with a parent.

HOW CAN MY STUDENTS PARTICIPATE IN THE RUBRIC ASSESSMENT PROCESS?

Most of the rubrics in this book are accompanied by a matching self-assessment checklist for your students. You've probably already discovered that once your students have a clear understanding of the particular skills you'll be looking for in their project or performance, they're more likely to produce better work. For this reason, it's a particularly good idea to show them the self-assessment checklist—or the rubric itself—even before they begin a task, so that they can refer to it while they work. Then, after they complete the task, have them use the same form to assess their work. Encourage your students to refer to the criteria and make any changes that could improve their work. As your students become familiar with rubrics, they can even create their own.

WHAT ARE SOME ADDITIONAL STRATEGIES FOR HELPING STUDENTS GIVE A TASK THEIR "BEST SHOT"?

Most of the assessment tasks in this book include planning forms or graphic organizers that will encourage them to write, draw, map, or outline their ideas before they begin to create their final work products. Whatever written or pictorial strategy your students use, it is likely to help them do a better job of thinking about how they might best tackle a task or project.

WHAT WILL HELP MY STUDENTS IMPROVE THEIR PERFORMANCES OVER TIME?

You will find suggestions for improving your students' skills on the TRY THIS! pages which follow most rubric assessment activities in this book. Also be sure to give your students plenty of class time to practice using the skills you plan to assess.

After scoring a performance task, you may want to have brief conferences with individual students to point out exactly what each needs to do to raise a specific skill to the next performance level. It's also important to have your students suggest ideas for improving their own work. Have them use a goal-setting sheet to list the areas of improvement they plan to focus on in their next writing assignment or project.

Name _____   Date _____

Goal Setting

Description of work/project: _____
_____

What I notice: _____
_____
_____
_____
_____

My goal: _____
_____

How can I determine each student's improvement over time?

First, it's a good idea to provide individual folders for each student's writing and reading assessments. Be sure to ask your students to write the date of each of the assessments on their paper before placing it in a folder. Once you begin recording your students' scores on your CLASS RECORD FORM (page 128), you will easily be able to compare their later performances with earlier ones. Then you can share this information—as well as the writing in the assessment folder—in a conference with a parent or student.

How do I inform parents about rubric assessments?

Set aside some time on Open School Night to show parents an example of a rubric while you point out the criteria and describe the various levels of achievement. You should also tell parents that rubrics are considered to be a valid form of evaluation and are currently used for assessing statewide reading and writing tests.

Parents will appreciate the specific, clear information they receive about their children's work. In a parent-teacher conference you might point to the level of the rubric that describes a student's essay and say, "Here's what Raymond was able to do." Then, after reading aloud the criteria that best describe the essay, you could point to the criteria at the next higher performance level and add, "And these are the skills he'll be working on next."

A rubric's criteria provide specific information that you can use when writing report cards. If you wanted to describe improvement in a student's social studies report writing, for example, you could refer to criteria in the rubric on page 99 and write something like this:

> "Amy's report writing has improved. Her reports now are organized around a central topic and developed with relevant details and information. She still requires some help using correct spelling, punctuation, and grammar."

Once you begin your rubric assessments, you will discover how well they connect evaluation and learning. With visions of what makes something worth a "4" in their heads, your students will try to create something even better than they had before. And by sharing rubrics with parents, you will gain partners who truly understand your reading and writing curriculum and the goals you have set for their children.

What Rubrics Do for Us

- focus and streamline curriculum planning

- make scoring of complex work products easier

- establish criteria for students' self-assessments

- identify steps students must take to improve a performance

- show growth in students' work over time

- offer specific information to share with parents

- provide criteria for writing report cards

How This Book Is Organized

A quick look at the CONTENTS page will show you the variety of genres this book provides for the assessment of typical reading and writing activities in 3–6 classrooms. These assessments are aimed at developing literacy capabilities required in real life learning situations; for example, writing personal essays, letters, and research reports; reading and analyzing short stories, novels, and nonfiction books; and creating content-area projects and presenting them to the class. Like many teachers, you probably also ask your students to write and read plays, poems, news articles, and speeches. Although this book does not include assessments for these genres, its final chapter will help you create your own.

PERSONAL EXPERIENCE ESSAYS

Influenced by the research of Donald Graves and Lucy Calkins as well as by my own work in the classroom, I believe that students write better when they write about experiences and subjects they know and care about. This book includes two assessments for personal writing:

- **On-Demand Tasks** require all students to respond *independently* to the same prompt or assignment. This assessment will show you what your students are able to do on their own with no feedback or editorial assistance. When conducted early in the school year, this assessment will help you determine what your students need to learn. Later in the school year, an on-demand task can show you change and growth.

⬧ **Workshop Writing Assessments** focus on student-selected topics for personal narratives and research essays that students develop in class over time with ongoing feedback from you and their classmates.

LETTER WRITING

With the advent of e-mail, letter writing is a genre that has made a comeback. Although your students may not have Internet access in school, you can be sure that many are e-mailing informal letters to friends and family members from their homes. This essential skill can be developed and improved through assessment.

In your classroom, there are many real-life opportunities for students to write friendly letters to pen pals as well as business letters to request materials or information. However, like many adults today, your students may not be familiar with current conventions for writing headings and closings of letters written for different purposes. The second chapter of this book provides a variety of assessment prompts and planning forms that will help your students become better letter writers.

READING COMPREHENSION

You've probably noticed that the focus today in schools across the country is on the assessment of reading, not with an eye for isolated skills but rather for learning how well students understand what they have read. To help them accomplish the challenging task of analyzing stories, this part of the book provides graphic organizers to plan the ways they will explain literary elements such as character, plot, theme, and setting.

In addition to assessing students' literary responses, we need to evaluate a variety of reading-related activities. For example, most of us ask our students to record the titles and authors of the books they read. These book lists can be analyzed by the students themselves to determine the extent of their reading as well the specific genres they have chosen. In many classrooms, students use literature logs to record their questions and personal reactions to a story. Literature logs can be analyzed by students and teachers to assess the frequency and the thoughtfulness of the written responses. When reading assessments are integrated with ongoing learning activities, you will find that they develop students' abilities and also work hand-in-hand with your teaching of reading.

CONTENT-AREA RESEARCH

There is a natural connection between reading, writing, speaking, and content-area research. A study of rainforests, for example, could involve the reading of nonfiction books, notetaking, and report writing. In addition, we often ask our students to create a project—such as a diorama—that requires accurate, artistic cut-outs, descriptive labels, and an oral presentation.

An integrated study has many benefits; it engages students in independent, valuable learning experiences. Yet it takes time, and at the end we must face the somewhat daunting task of assessing the rich variety of work products our students have created. Just what is it that makes a report, a diorama, or a presentation excellent, good, satisfactory, or poor? This is the question that a rubric helps us answer by providing criteria for each performance level.

Once you become familiar with the rubrics in this book, you will easily be able to create a rubric for assessing the work products of a content-area study in your own classroom.

How to Use This Book

Use the TABLE OF CONTENTS to locate a chapter that describes the assessment of a learning activity that fits your present needs.

You will notice that they are organized into the following sections:

1 An INTRODUCTION describes the genre.

2 IN ADVANCE recommends materials you should prepare—such as writing a prompt or photocopying materials and forms—before you begin the assessment. For an on-demand assessment, this section will also suggest the approximate amount of time you should allow.

3 PREPARE YOUR STUDENTS outlines information to give your students prior to the assessment.

4 CONDUCT THE ASSESSMENT provides explanations that you will need to give your students during the assessment and tells you which forms to distribute. Following all assessments, of course, you should collect the students' self-assessment forms and work products.

5 A TRY THIS! page at the end of each chapter lists genre-related ideas and materials that will help your students improve their skills.

Personal Experience Essays

An assessment early in the school year shows us what our new students need to learn about good writing—the kind of information we need for planning our writing mini-lessons. Baseline samples are also valuable, because they provide evidence of change and growth when we compare them with later assessments taken at mid-year and in June. When gathering benchmark writing samples, it's important to have all students respond to the same prompt. You should select a different prompt for each follow-up assessment.

As writing teachers we've learned that our students usually write better when they can write about meaningful personal experiences or about subjects that are interesting and important to them. To provide a common writing topic for all your students, you can create your own prompt or select any one of the following. Write the prompt on the chalkboard or make photocopies.

Suggested Prompts

Write about someone you think is special—a friend, a pet, a family member, a teacher, or anyone else. In your essay be sure to include:

- a description of the special person or pet
- the reason why that person or pet is special
- specific details, examples, thoughts, and feelings
- a satisfying ending

2 Write about an event or experience in your life that you'll never forget. In your essay be sure to include:

- a description of the incident or experience
- any feelings you had, such as happiness, fear, pride, anger, surprise, or disappointment
- specific details, descriptions, dialogue, and thoughts
- a satisfying ending

3 Write about a time when someone taught you something new or a time when you taught someone else. In your essay be sure to include:

- what the "lesson" was
- the reason for the lesson
- the person who did the teaching
- what was learned from the lesson
- specific details, descriptions, dialogue, thoughts, and feelings
- a satisfying ending

Adapted from the New York State Language Arts Test Sampler, 1998

4 Write about a perfect day. In your essay be sure to include:

- a description of the perfect day
- any feelings you had, such as pride, surprise, happiness, or satisfaction
- specific details, descriptions, dialogue, and thoughts
- a satisfying ending

In Advance

- Set aside plenty of time—perhaps as much as an hour to an hour and a half—for your students to write a rough draft, edit the draft, and write a final copy. It's important to provide an activity break after about 40 minutes or so.

- On a chart or chalkboard, write the prompt you have selected. Make photocopies of the planning form on page 32 for the class.

- Adapt the self-assessment checklists on pages 33–35 to match your students' abilities and experiences. Then make photocopies for your class.

- Make an overhead transparency or photocopies of the rubric on page 36.

- Provide lined paper for writing rough drafts and final copies.

- Copy the STEPS FOR WRITING (below) onto a chart or make enough photocopies for the class.

PREPARE YOUR STUDENTS

- Show your students the rubric you will use to assess their writing. Explain the criteria and encourage questions and discussion.

- Distribute the self-assessment forms, and explain that these checklists will show them the changes they need to make to improve their first drafts.

- Show your students how to use a caret (∧) to add words and a deletion mark (Ϙ) to remove words. Point out that by skipping lines as they write their rough drafts they will have extra spaces for inserting additional words and sentences later on.

CONDUCT THE ASSESSMENT

- Read the writing prompt aloud to your students, and answer any questions they may have about the task.

- Read aloud the following information:

STEPS FOR WRITING

1 Think about what you will write. Make notes of your ideas on your planning sheet.

2 Write a rough draft. Leave a space between each line of writing so you can add or change words.

3 Reread your writing to see if you have included all your important ideas.

4 Read and complete your self-assessment checklists. Make any changes in your draft that you think will improve your writing.

5 Proofread to correct any errors. Then recopy your revised story onto lined paper.

✻ Distribute the form MY WRITING PLAN and the paper that students will use for their first drafts and have them write their name and date on each page.

✻ Distribute the MY WRITING ORGANIZATION AND DEVELOPMENT Checklist on page 33 and the EDITING CHECKLIST on page 34.

✻ Remind your students to write their name and the date on the draft as well as on the paper they will use for writing their final copies.

FOLLOWING AN ASSESSMENT

✻ Collect all writings—final copies and drafts as well as prompts.

✻ Use the rubric on page 36 to review the criteria you will be looking for in your students' writing.

✻ Read each student's paper. Refer to the rubric to determine which level describes the student's writing. Write the score on the paper.

IMPORTANT NOTE: Some papers may appear to meet most, but not all, of the criteria for a particular level. Ask yourself, "Which best describes this writing?" Go with your impression! If you're stuck, add a plus or minus sign after a score.

✻ Record the date and each student's developmental stage or score on a CLASS RECORD FORM (page 128).

Try Your Hand at Scoring Writing!

The following is a rubric selected to score the prompt, "Write about a time when someone taught you how to do something or you taught someone else." Use the rubric to score the grade 4 student examples that follow it. (Keep in mind that the writings may not be an exact match for a particular level. Use a plus or minus sign, if necessary, and trust your impressions.)

In the margins you'll find notes that describe the way another teacher scored each one.

Key Elements of Proficient Writing

Idea Development   The topic is fully developed with relevant information. Details, examples, descriptions, or anecdotes support and clarify ideas.

Organization   The information is organized in a logical order. It has an introduction that engages the reader and a satisfying ending.

Language Usage   The writing has lively and descriptive language. Precise verbs and specific nouns explain and clarify the information.

Sentence Structure   Sentences vary in type and length.

Mechanics and Conventions   There are few errors in punctuation, capitalization, and paragraphing. Sentences are complete (few or no run-ons or fragments).

Scoring Levels

The key elements are evident:

(3 points)   to a high degree

(2 points)   to a satisfactory degree

(1 point)   to a limited degree

(0 points)   No key elements are evident, or errors in paragraphs, sentence structure, spelling, or mechanics interfere with the reader's ability to understand the text.

SAMPLE 1

One time when someone taught me somthin was when I went sking for the first time. My ski Instructors name was scott he worked at a mountain called Beaver Creek it is in Collorado. I went a magic carpet and went down a little hill. and I kept falling so I thought I stunk my ski instuctor said not to give up.

Score 1

Explanation:

(lines 1–3)   The introductory sentence states the topic.

(lines 4–8)   There is an attempt to develop the topic through a list of details (instructor's name, location, mention of falling while going down a hill) without descriptions or development of ideas.

(lines 9–10)   Ending: instructor's advice. The writing shows simple statements and everyday vocabulary.

Several errors in spelling, capitalization, and punctuation do not significantly interfere with a reader's ability to understand the text.

SAMPLE 2

My friend taught me how to do an oragami balloon. Her name is Payal. Some of the parts were hard but most of them were easy. She taught me really well. Then she taught me how to do a crane but I forgot. The balloon was easy to remember because I did it over and over. Now I can teach other people.

Score 2

Explanation:

(line 1)   An introductory sentence states the topic.

(lines 2, 3, 4)   Development of the topic is minimal. There is no description of the lesson other than "some parts were hard but most of them were easy."

(lines 4, 5)   The last sentence sums up the experience. "Now I can teach other people."

The writing uses simple and compound sentences and everyday language correctly. There are no errors in spelling and capitalization. Periods are used correctly.

Score 1+

Explanation:

(line 1)   Introductory sentence states the topic.

(lines 2–10)   The topic is fully developed with examples of the writer's progress in learning to roller-blade. Simple sentences and everyday language are used to develop ideas.

     Multiple errors in spelling, punctuation, grammar, and paragraphing frequently interfere with the reader's ability to understand the text.

Note to teachers: This is a tough paper to score because of errors in the mechanics and conventions of writing. Scores probably will range from 1 to 2-. A major purpose of the assessment is to discover exactly what we need to teach a student, and this paper makes our lessons evident!

SAMPLE 3

My brother tought me how to roller blade. I ask him and he said yes. We went outside and he held me up. I fell down sometimes but I got it soon. I ferst Roller bladed in a park then in front of my house. It was the socand week. I was finaly Roller blading up and down the stret and I was happy. But I whanted to now some triks to. I ask him he tought me how to do a turn twist but codint do it so he ought me something els. It was called foot turn. and I did it I was so happy I could do it and I wanted learn more he said now I will tech you how to to some thing real fun. I said yes we had to go down a hill it was dangeros but yes I did It was fun I did not get heart at all my brother di it and he did not get heart eathe.

SAMPLE 4

Last year, I was in third grade. Just that day I had finished learning the letters **E m m** and **a**. I relized I was able to write my sister's name! I got off the bus and ran into the building, and up the elevator. I sat Emma down in the kitchen. Although she was only in first grade, I was determend to teach her how to write her name in script. First, I took a Sharpie marker and wrote it clearly and cleanly. Then, Emma picked it up and wrote **E mmm mm o**. NO! I screamed and made a fist pointing it towards her head. Quickly I put my fist down. I held her small hand in mine and together we wrote, **Emma**. "You did it!" I cried. I had taught her almost exactly the same way my teacher had. I saw a broad smile spread across he face, as she rushed to tell our baby sitter. I had lost my temper but, like all good teachers I quickly recoverd. I felt proud. I had made me, my sister and my baby sitter all feel proud. My sister had learned some thing new, I had taught her, and my baby-sitter hade the pleasure of watching my sister and me learn.

Score 3

Explanation:

(lines 1–5) Introduction is fully developed.

(lines 6–13) Relevant information, details, dialogue, and anecdotes fully develop the topic in a lively, interesting way. The language is descriptive ("...a broad smile spread across her face"); precise verbs (realized, determined, screamed, pointing, spread, rushed, recovered) make the writer's meaning clear.

(lines 13–16) A fully developed, effective ending describes the outcomes of the teaching experience.

Sentences vary in structure and length. Although ideas and actions are logically organized, errors in paragraphing are evident. There are few errors in spelling or mechanics.

Score 3+ or 4

Reader's Comments:

Focused on the task. Develops topic well with clear descriptions. "He held on to the back of the seat pushed me and I was off." Uses precise language: "feel the wind rushing into my face. I wobble, I fell, and I was crying and had a bloody knee." Writes language that flows: "I could feel the bumps under me and the wind once again in my face. I went flying and I never fell again." Creates a satisfying ending: "Thanks to my dad now I can ride anywhere I want." There are few errors in punctuation, capitalization, and spelling.

I remember the first time I rode my bike.... My dad taught me. He held on to the back of the seat pushed me and I was off. I could feel the wind rushing into my face. I wobble, I fell, and I was cring and had a bloody knee. My dad took me inside to clean me up and put a bandade on my knee. Then we went back outside to try again. My dad held on to the back of the seat and off I was again. I could feel the bumps under me and the wind once again in my face. I went flying and I never fell again.

Thanks to my dad now I can ride anywhere I want.

One day my brother had a playdate with one of his friends. So I decieded to go along with him. Then my brother's friend's sister was there. She taught me how to do a stich with string, it was called "Candy stripe." it was a very pretty stich. So the day after, I went to school and taught my friends how to do it. This is how I tolled them how to do it. I knew everybody knew how to do the stich chineese store case so I told them just to keep doing that. Then I showed them an exsample with my string then my friends started understanding and soon after evreybody knew how to do "Candy stripe."

Score 2

Reader's comments:

Attempts to focus on the task after first several lines. Had difficulty explaining a "Candy stripe" stitch. Run-on sentences, several errors in punctuation and capitalization. No paragraphs. Story events are logically sequenced, however.

A long time ago I couldn't hit a base ball. So one day my Dad said "lets practice hitting a baseball." My Dad. was going to teach me.

So the next day was Saturday We went to the park and my dad pitched some to me. A few minuetes passed and I still couldn't hit, he pitched the next one I swung and I missed by far then my Mom showed up and she pitched my Dad helped me swing, I hit it!! I yelled. It was a grounder right back to my mom.

My Dad went back to pitching and my mom was catcher I swung and I hit it that is how I learned to hit a baseball.

Score 3

Reader's comments:

Focused on task. Introductory paragraph uses dialogue and provides necessary information. Logically organized and sequenced descriptions of learning to bat a baseball. Word choice is adequate. Events organized into paragraphs. Ending sums up the experience. "That is how I learned to hit a baseball." Several errors in punctuation. Run-on sentence in paragraph 2. Uses language appropriately.

Assessing Writing Within the Writing Workshop

A workshop is a process-oriented, hands-on approach that gives students choices and opportunities to interact while they write. If you already use this approach, then you know how important ongoing feedback is for the development of writing. You also know that crafting a piece from rough draft to completed work may take several days or even weeks. On pages 32–35, you'll find planning forms and self-assessment checklists, which will help your students improve their own work.

Here are a few tips that will help you assess workshop writing:

❋ Focus initially on the content of the writing and assess writing conventions afterwards.

❋ If a typo appears in the final copy, look at the way the word is spelled in the rough draft. If the word is written correctly in the draft, ignore the typo.

❋ My annotations explain my thinking as I read the students' essays. Of course, you will have your own ideas. You need not annotate your students' papers. However, you may find it helpful to jot down qualities you notice on a sticky-paper note and place it on the page. These notes will be useful for mini-lesson ideas and for your writing conferences with individual students.

Select a rubric from pages 36–39 to assess workshop writings. If you teach grade 6 be sure to use RUBRIC #3 on page 38 for this assessment.

Unlike the on-demand writing assessments you just considered, the following essays were developed over time through a workshop approach. After receiving feedback on their drafts in conferences with the teacher and classmates, students revised and edited their writing. If you use a workshop approach with your students, you can expect to see higher scores for workshop writings than for "on-demand" assessments.

Look at the ways the following writing exemplars from grades 3 through 6 have been scored using the criteria in the rubric on page 38 Your scores may not always agree with the scores (levels) I have shown for the writings. In fact, small differences can be expected because holistic scoring relies on teachers' impressions. For this reason, many state tests resolve scoring discrepancies by having two teachers independently rate the same writings. The sum of their scores for each key element then becomes the final score for each essay. Another easy solution is to add a plus or minus sign to a score. Also, now that you've had some practice, be sure to add your own comments to the "sidebars."

NOTE: It is also useful to have these exemplars to use as benchmarks when students begin work on designing rubrics collaboratively (see page 110).

Writing Exemplars Grades 3–6

THE EDGEWOOD FAIR

Tick, Tick, Tick, Tick....tick....tick...."And the number is ..." Everyone standing at the wheel of fortune booth at the Edgewood Fair on May seventh held their breaths. They stared at the kelly green and white wheel with the numbers one through sixteen on it as it spun slower and slower. Their eyes were glued to the wheel. You could feel the mounting excitement. People bit their fingernails and cracked their knuckles. They paid no attention to the shrieks of laughter and noisy yells that came from the rest of the fair which was held on the blacktop behind them.

The wheel ticked its last tick.

"Number seven!" Sallie Sills yelped out gleefully, "That's my number!" She collected her prize - a picture of Garfield on a field of bright blue aluminum foil - and went off happily with whomever she had come with.

This was one favorite of the many booths found at the fair on that sunny Saturday. The theme of the fair was The Wizard of Oz and you could see pictures of the much-famous Dorothy brightly painted everywhere.

The kids were lucky to be there, and they knew it. Happiness and excitement was everywhere; on a little kid's face when buying a balloon; the joy of gooey cotton candy sticking everywhere showed on kids' faces as they took huge bites, letting the sweetness disintegrate in their mouths - only to take another bite, bigger than the first.

The red and white striped booths combining with the green and yellow balloons made a carnival-like atmosphere. The popcorn, ice cream, hot dogs, and barbecued chicken yakitori added the most delicious smells imaginable to the atmosphere.

There were dart booths, basketball booths, and booths where you just won a prize. There was a prizewalk and a plantshop - for the next day was Mother's Day.

Everyone hated to go, but at three o'clock the booths came down, and the leftover food was taken home. The air hung heavy with the feeling that is always there after a fair is finished - not depression, but wistfulness, especially for the sixth graders. It was their last year at Edgewood, their last true school fair. They'd always be able to visit, but it would never be quite the same. They stayed as long as possible, and when they finally had to leave they walked slowly, looking back frequently at the collapsing booths and wilted plants under the hot yellow afternoon sun. The smell of stale popcorn and burnt barbecue sauce still hung in the air.

Courtesy of Jean Little, former grade 6 teacher, Edgewood School

Proficient (Level 5)

Annotations for "The Edgewood Fair" (grade 6)

para. 1: Specific sights, sounds, and action draw the reader's interest.

para. 2: Deliberate repetition of "tick" creates suspense.

para. 3: Dialogue and description of prize show the joy of winning.

para. 4: the time, setting, and theme of the fair

para. 5–7: Sensory details—smells, tastes, and descriptions— show the pleasures of the fair.

para. 8: Sensory details—actions, sights, and smells—convey a "wistful" mood ("…they walked slowly, looking back frequently at the collapsing booths….The smell of stale popcorn…hung in the air").

Summary: The topic is fully developed with relevant, interesting information. Sentence variety, supportive information, and precise word choices create an exceptionally clear and interesting narrative. This essay has "voice"—it reflects the thoughts and feelings of the writer. The narrative is organized in paragraphs with an effective introduction and ending. There are few errors in writing conventions.

Your Thoughts?

The Great Restaurant Battle

"Joey, don't antaganize him," my mother said from across the table. I was in Florida visiting my grandmother, with my mom, my very big brother Joe, and my sister Gloria. Any way, we were at a restaurant eating lunch.

All day, I wasn't in harmony with my brother but this had to top it off.

I whined to my mother, "I can't eat no more. I'm chuck full."

My grandmother said to me, "One more bite and then you don't have to eat anymore," which was better than finishing it all. I was so full one bite felt like eating the whole thing

all over again. So I was there chewing and chewing and chewing. "Man this thing doesn't want to go down my throat, there's no more room."

Meanwhile, my stomach was saying to my brain, "No room. No room."

"Oh, is poor little Jon going to cry?"

"Joe, quit when you're ahead."

"Is that a threat I hear coming out of thyest mouth?"

"Will you two cut it out, all the people in this place are going to be looking at us," my mom scolded. I totally ignored what my mother said and I loaded my straw with a perfect spit ball. I sought

Example of a fourth grader's workshop writing (Score 4)

my target, Joey's mouth. When he opened, pow! But it didn't go according to plans. I took a deep breath, held it and applied the straw to my mouth. The second I was going to fire, my grandmother blocked the straw. I was turning blue. Finally, she took it out of my mouth.

"Who tought you how to do that?", my grandmother yelled.

"My father".

My grandmother almost chokied up all the water melon she had in her mouth.

"Wait until I get a hold of him.

Joe was laughing. I said to Joe in an exasperated way; "You might "of" won the battle but the war is yet to come.

Capable (Level 4)

Annotations for "The Great Restaurant Battle" (grade 4)

title: draws the reader's interest and focuses on the topic

para. 1–2: Dialogue introduces the setting and the characters.

para. 3–5: Examples describe and develop the writer's problem [too full to eat any more]. Deliberate repetition makes the chewing problem clear.

para. 6–9: Realistic, humorous dialogue shows the "battle" between the brothers.

para. 9: Strong verbs—ignored, loaded, sought, applied, blocked—clarify the action.

para. 10–13: Realistic descriptions and dialogue create humor.

para. 14: The ending is satisfying. It maintains the humor of the piece.

Summary: The narrative uses realistic characters, dialogue, and actions to create humor. Events, actions, and descriptions are developed with details that contribute to the humor and draw the reader's interest. The writing shows paragraph sense, complete sentences, sentence variety, and effective verb choices. Spelling and capitalization are correct. Grammatical errors are used deliberately to create authentic dialogue. A few punctuation errors appear in dialogues.

Your Thoughts?

Satisfactory (Level 3)

Annotations for "Schef Grandmadee" (grade 4)

para. 1: Paragraph draws the reader's attention and introduces the main idea of the narrative.

lines 4–17: [Conversation with grandmother as she cooks] Realistic dialogue shows how fried dough is made. The dialogue lacks narrative breaks.

page 2, para. 1: Explains the setting and characters.

para. 2: Description is effective (grandmother bringing dinner to the table); uses specifics ("two pots, one big one filled with sauce and one filled with ravioles").

para. 3: Ending is satisfying ("After the Catholic prayer, my grandmother said, 'Now we can eat, manga'").

Summary: The main topic of the essay—grandmother as cook—is developed with relevant, interesting information and organized logically in paragraphs. Dialogue is overused with only a few breaks to identify speakers ("I said" or "she said"). Errors in spelling and punctuation do not interfere with the reader's ability to understand the text. The ending is effective.

Your Thoughts?

Schef Grandmadee

"MMMMMMMmmm" I said, the most awsome aroma came from the kichen. I went in there and saw my grandmother cooking., I asked her what it was

"It's fried dough," she said.

"How does it taste?"

"Here try," she said.

"Eeeewweweww this tastes disgusting!"

"That's because you're missing the main ingredient".

"What is it?" I said.

"Sugar."

"Mmmmmm, this is the greatest," I said.

Can you show me how to make fried dough so I can do it home?"

"Sure. First you take some flour and water and put the flour on the table. Then put a little water in gradually and squish it together intill it becomes soft like pizza dough.

Usually my whole family which includes my father, mother, brothers, sister, aunt, uncle, grandmother, and grandfather all eat on a Sunday or on holidays at my grandparent's house.

Then when everybody was talking very loud, my grandmother came walking in from the kitchen with two pots, *one big* one filled with sauce ~~big pot~~ and one filled with ravioles. Then everone stopped talking and looked at my granmother she put the pots on the table.

Then she said, "Take some." everyone started to take some but they didn"t eat yet. "Now we Christine has to say Grace," said my grandmother. After the Catholic prayer, my grandmother said, "Now we can eat, manga."

When I had a black eye

When I was five I went skiing with an instructor. I went down a hill and when I got down I fell. Someone skied over my face. My dad said I had a black eye. He took me to the hospital. The person at the hospital said I had a black eye and my dad already had a black eye and my dads eye was healing. The next day I had to go to School with a black eye.

Developing (Level 2)

"When I had a black eye" (grade 3)

lines 1–3: Introduction presents the main idea.

lines 4–9: Information is not developed with opinions, details, or explanations; essay does not explain how dad got his black eye.

Summary: The writing shows a focused topic that is organized with an introduction followed by a series of events. The ending is the last event. The writing is minimally developed with few supportive details, personal reactions, or descriptions. There are few errors in spelling, punctuation, and capitalization. Paragraphing skills are not demonstrated.

Your Thoughts?

Developing (Level 2-)

Annotations for "Christmasis in the city" (grade 3)

lines 1–3: Introductory sentence states the topic.

lines 4–6: "Lists" four facts about the carriage ride that are not developed with opinions, examples, or explanations.

Summary: The topic is minimally developed in a single paragraph with little supportive description or information. The writing lacks "voice"—a liveliness that draws a reader's interest. There are few errors in spelling, punctuation, and capitalization. Paragraphing skills are not demonstrated.

Your Thoughts?

Christmasis in the city

This christmas vacation I went to this city and my mom and I went in a carriage. It was a nice view. It took about sixty ty minutes. We went around Central Park. It was cold.

My Special Place
Grade 4

My Special P.
Score 1
My Special place where
I like the most is the
Slatterys house there
shining stare in high
school basketball they live
right nexks house
to me there Chuck & Chris
they where in the Finals.
We watch T.V at there
house. I like there dog
Regis it plays dead.
Chris & Chuck are funny.

Novice (Level 1)

My Special Place (grade 4)

lines 1–3: Introduction presents the topic.

lines 4–12: The writer attempts to develop the topic, but multiple errors in spelling, sentence structure, punctuation, capitalization, and paragraphing significantly interfere with the reader's ability to understand the text.

Your Thoughts?

Organizing the Writing Workshop

Because finding a writing topic can be a daunting task for all writers, many teachers should encourage students to draw ideas from their own experiences and interests. You can help your students get started by offering them writing prompts such as the following:

A place I like is...   One of my favorite...
I'll never forget...   I was really proud when...
I was scared when...

After they select a topic, have them use MY WRITING PLAN on page 32 to make notes for their essays. This prewriting graphic organizer may be completed as a homework assignment so that when writing time begins, they will know just where to start, making the best use of their workshop time. For more tips on organizing a workshop, read *Teaching Writing: A Workshop Approach* by Adele Fiderer (Scholastic Professional Books, 1994).

Name _____   Date _____

My Writing Plan

Directions: Use this form to help you think about your writing ideas.

1 My story is about: _____

_____

2 Ideas for titles: _____

_____ [Check the one you like best]

3 How my story will begin: _____

_____

_____

_____

4 Events and ideas I will write about in the main part of my story:

_____

_____

_____

_____

_____

5 How my story will end: _____

_____

_____

40 Rubrics & Checklists to Assess Reading and Writing Scholastic Professional Books

Name _____ Date _____

Title _____

My Writing Organization and Development

	Yes	**No**
1. My writing has an interesting introduction that will make someone want to keep reading.	☐	☐
2. I write events and ideas in an order that makes sense.	☐	☐
3. I use details, descriptions, examples, and quotations that focus on my topic and develop my story.	☐	☐
4. My title fits my story and draws a reader's interest.	☐	☐
5. My ending ties things up.	☐	☐

My Sentences:

	Yes	**No**
◉ are not run-ons (run-ons have two sentences together without a period or a connecting word)	☐	☐
◉ begin with a capital letter	☐	☐
◉ use commas and quotation marks where needed	☐	☐
◉ end with a period, question mark, or exclamation point	☐	☐
◉ are grouped in paragraphs, with a new paragraph for each change of subject or speaker	☐	☐
◉ use strong verbs that show the action (*squeal, tumbled*)	☐	☐
◉ use specific nouns that create pictures in the reader's mind (*Tootsie Roll, dalmatians, autumn*)	☐	☐

Name _____ Date _____

Editing Checklist
(Upper Elementary)

Read your writing to see if you should answer **Yes** or **No** to each question. If your answer to a question is No, make the appropriate correction.

	Yes	No
1. Did I use complete sentences (no fragments)?	☐	☐
2. Does each sentence begin with a capital letter and end with a period, question mark, or exclamation point?	☐	☐
3. Did I check to see that I have no run-on sentences?	☐	☐
4. Are my sentences logically organized into paragraphs?	☐	☐
5. Did I check my spelling and make corrections?	☐	☐
6. Did I capitalize the names of people, places, and titles?	☐	☐
7. Did I use quotation marks around spoken words?	☐	☐
8. Did I use commas correctly?	☐	☐
9. Did I use apostrophes for contractions?	☐	☐
10. Did I use apostrophes to show possession?	☐	☐

40 Rubrics & Checklists to Assess Reading and Writing Scholastic Professional Books

Name _____ Date _____

Title _____

A Writing Checklist
(Grade 3)

1. I read my writing to myself to see if it made sense. ☐

2. I used specific words to make my writing clearer. ☐

Examples:

sprinted	**whispered**	**Hershey bar**	**cheese sandwich**
∧ ~~ran~~	∧ ~~said~~	∧ ~~candy~~	∧ ~~lunch~~

3. I read my story again to see where to stop for ☐

periods .   **question marks ?**   **exclamation points !**

4. I crossed out extra words (*and, then*) that I didn't need. ☐

5. I used capital letters:

at the beginning of each sentence ☐

for the first letter of each name ☐

for the word *I* ☐

6. I looked for words that might be misspelled and tried to correct them. ☐

7. I recopied my draft. ☐

Rubric #1 for Evaluating On-Demand Writing Tasks

Key Elements	Evaluative Criteria
◉ **Task**	Fulfills the requirements of the task.
◉ **Idea Development**	Develops relevant ideas and events clearly and fully. Uses details, examples, and anecdotes to support ideas and clarify information.
◉ **Organization**	Organizes information logically. Uses appropriate transitions to sequence ideas. Includes an effective introduction and ending.
◉ **Language Usage**	Uses language fluently and engages the reader. Chooses words that make the writing clear and understandable. Varies sentence length and structure.
◉ **Mechanics**	Makes few errors in basic language conventions.

4	**Capable**	All key elements are well developed.
3	**Satisfactory**	The key elements are adequately developed.
2	**Developing**	The story conveys meaning, although some or all key elements are partially developed. Errors do not interfere with the reader's ability to understand the text.
1	**Novice**	No key elements are developed, or errors interfere with the reader's ability to understand the text.

40 Rubrics & Checklists to Assess Reading and Writing

Scholastic Professional Books

Rubric #2 for Evaluating Workshop Writing

Key Elements of Proficient Writing

Level 3

Idea Development	Develops the topic clearly and fully with relevant information. Uses details, descriptions, and anecdotes to explain and clarify information.
Organization	Logically organizes ideas in paragraphs. Has an effective introduction (e.g., action, dialogue, an unusual image, a question) and a satisfying ending.
Language Usage	Uses lively and descriptive language. Uses precise verbs (*climbed, rode, whispered*). Varies sentence length and structure. Writing has a lively "voice" that engages the reader
Mechanics	Makes few errors in basic language conventions.

Level 2

Idea Development	Develops the topic with adequate, relevant information, and details.
Organization	Presents information in a logical order with few or no paragraphs. Begins with the first event in an incident or experience. Has a closing statement (*That was one of the best games I ever saw*).
Language Usage	Uses appropriate language. Provides the basic information with little elaboration or sentence variety (*Yesterday I went to a baseball game. The Yankees were playing Baltimore. Baltimore was up*).
Mechanics	Uses capitalization, question marks, and periods appropriately most of the time. Errors do not interfere with comprehension of the topic.

Level 1

Idea Development	Attempts to develop the topic. Provides few details to support ideas. Topic is broad with no focus or guiding theme (**My Trip to California; All About Me**).
Organization	Attempts to sequence information. Some information may be omitted or out of order. Endings may be the last in a "list" of experiences.
Language Usage	Uses simple sentences and vocabulary. Grammar may be incorrect.
Mechanics	Uses capital letters, question marks, periods inconsistently.

Rubric #3 for Evaluating Workshop Writing

Key Elements	Evaluative Criteria
Idea Development	The topic/task is fully developed with relevant information. Details, examples, descriptions, or anecdotes support and clarify ideas.
Organization	The information is organized in a logical order. It has an introduction that engages the reader, and it has a satisfying ending.
Language Usage	The writing has lively and descriptive language. Precise verbs and specific nouns explain and clarify the information. Sentences vary in types and length.
Mechanics and Conventions	There are few errors in punctuation, capitalization, and paragraphing. Sentences are complete (few or no run-ons or fragments).

Scoring Levels

The key elements are evident:

5	points	to an exceptionally high degree
4	points	to a moderately high degree
3	points	to a satisfactory degree
2	points	to a limited degree
1	point	No key elements are adequately developed, or errors in spelling or mechanics interfere with the reader's ability to understand the text.

40 Rubrics & Checklists to Assess Reading and Writing   Scholastic Professional Books

Name _____   Date _____

Title/Topic _____   Score _____

Writing Rubric #4 to Share With Kids

Key Elements	Evaluative Criteria
Idea Development	The topic/task is fully developed with relevant information. Details, examples, descriptions, or anecdotes support and clarify ideas.
Organization	The information is organized in a logical order. It has an introduction that engages the reader and a satisfying ending.
Language Usage	The writing has lively and descriptive language. Precise verbs and specific nouns explain and clarify the information. Sentences vary in types and length.
Mechanics and Conventions	There are few errors in punctuation, capitalization, and paragraphing. Sentences are complete (few or no run-ons or fragments).

Scoring Levels
The key elements are evident:

4 points   to a high degree

3 points   to a satisfactory degree

2 points   to a limited degree

1 point   No key elements are adequately developed, or errors in spelling and mechanics interfere with the reader's ability to understand the text.

Comments: _____

_____

_____

This rubric is designed for teachers to personalize for kids; they can return it attached to the student's writing.

TRY THIS!

STRATEGIES TO BUILD YOUR STUDENTS' WRITING SKILLS

⚙ Set aside class time at least three days each week for your students to write for 40 to 60 minutes.

⚙ Have your students develop a list of topics that they know and care about. Tell them to refer to this list when they need a writing idea.

⚙ To help your students improve their first-draft writings, post a sign-up list for writing conferences with you. For more tips on conferring and revising, read *Teaching Writing: A Workshop Approach* (Scholastic, 1993).

⚙ Plan mini-lessons that focus on the elements of good writing. See *25 Mini-Lessons for Teaching Writing* by Adele Fiderer (1997) and *Brighten Up Boring Beginnings and Other Quick Writing Lessons* by Laura Robb (1999), both published by Scholastic Professional Books, for student activity forms.

⚙ Make additional copies of the writing self-assessment checklists on pages 33–35 for your students to use throughout the year.

⚙ Set aside time for your students to read aloud their writing to the class. Encourage their classmates to ask the writer questions and offer suggestions for improving a draft.

⚙ Photocopy examples of good writing onto an overhead transparency for a class discussion of what makes each one "good."

⚙ Ask your students to share the word pictures and beautiful language that they find in the books they read. Create a Word Wall using pieces of chart paper to keep a running list of notable language use.

⚙ Have your students keep writers' notebooks—places where they can record ideas for writing as well as examples of good writing they find in literature. Ralph Fletcher's *Breathing In, Breathing Out* (Heinemann, 1996) and *Hey World, Here I Am* (Harper Trophy, 1991), Jean Little's fictional account of a girl who keeps a writer's notebook, will encourage notebook writing.

⚙ Stock your classroom library with memoirs by authors of children's novels to help your students find the meaningful stories in their own lives.

Great Memoirs

A Girl From Yamhill
by Beverly Cleary

Boy
by Roald Dahl

Childtimes
by Eloise Greenfield

My Own Story
by Jean Fritz

Circle of Quiet
by Madeleine L'Engle

Little by Little
by Jean Little

Always Grandma
by Vaunda Michaux Nelson

But I'll Be Back Again: An Album
by Cynthia Rylant

No Star Nights
by Anna Egan Smucker

Letter Writing

You have probably already discovered how effectively letter writing can be used to support your curriculum. Pen-pal letters, for example, will connect your students to people in other communities. Letters to a favorite author may bring a response that keeps the student reading that author's works. And letters of inquiry—which are business letters—can be useful for obtaining information they need for a science or geography study. Most students like letter writing because it's a short, manageable task, and the letter often needs to be no more than a page long. But perhaps the most important reason that children like to write letters is because of the response it produces. Who doesn't love to receive a letter in the mail?

> Bay Haven School of
> Basics Plus
> 2901 Tamiami Circle
> Sarasota, Fl 34235
> November 13, 1998
>
> Dear Mrs. Burns,
>
> Thank you for coming back to fifth grade, but I was kinda absent. I remember you from last year & you were great. I loved how you talked about "starting strong" and to "show not tell". Thank you for teaching us about transitions and how to mack our writing more interesting.
>
> My class last year picked Casey Mabney and me to visit the young Author's at U.S.F. New College. We meet another author who wrote The Great Kapok Tree. It made me one step foward to being a better writer.
>
> Sincerly,
> Jason Akal

Courtesy of Mary Alice Hratko, grade 5 teacher, Bay Haven School of Basics Plus

You will find this assessment easier at the beginning if all your students write a letter for the same purpose. Decide whether your students will write friendly letters or business letters. Then select one of the following prompts or create one to meet your own students' needs and interests.

❁ Write to a friend or family member you haven't seen in a while. In your letter be sure to include:

● a reason for your writing
● specific details and examples of events or experiences that you want to share with that person
● an ending that will make the person want to write back to you

✸ Write a thank-you letter to someone who has given you a gift or who has been helpful to you. In your letter be sure to include:

- the reason for your writing
- specific details that explain why you appreciate the gift or the person's assistance
- a closing statement that sums up your appreciation

✸ Write a business letter to Pizza Napoli, a frozen pizza company, suggesting ways they could improve their pizzas. Their address is 2051 Main Street, San Francisco, CA 96438. In your letter be sure to include:

- the reason for your writing
- specific ways to improve the pizzas
- a closing statement

✸ Write a letter to the Perfect Pencil Company, complaining that their $14.00 electronic pencil sharpener is too noisy to use in class. The company's address is 2 Main Street, Dobbs Ferry, New York 10522. In your letter be sure to include:

- the reason why you are writing
- specific details telling what happens when you use the pencil sharpener
- a closing statement about what you would like the company to do.

✸ Invite Mrs. Emily Sansone, a neighbor and writer, to give your class tips on how to get their writing published. Her address is 9 Acorn Street, Minneapolis, Minnesota 10039. In your letter be sure to include:

- the reason why you are writing
- some questions or topics that would interest your classmates
- a closing statement

IN ADVANCE

✸ Make photocopies of the appropriate planning form and self-assessment checklist, which you'll find on the following pages.

✸ Make photocopies of one of the EDITING CHECKLISTS on page 34 or 35 for the class.

- Photocopy TIPS FOR WRITING EFFECTIVE LETTERS (page 44) or copy the information onto a chart.

- Have lined paper available for students to write their drafts and final copies.

- Write the prompt on the chalkboard or make photocopies.

PREPARE YOUR STUDENTS

- Share the appropriate letter-writing rubric with your students.

- Distribute copies of the appropriate planning form and discuss it with your class.

- Distribute copies of the Self-Assessment Checklist your students will use.

- Read aloud and discuss TIPS FOR WRITING EFFECTIVE LETTERS.

- Allow 45 minutes for students to plan, write, and edit their drafts.

- Have students complete their Self-Assessment Checklists and write their final copies.

FOLLOWING AN ASSESSMENT

- Collect all writings—final copies and drafts as well as prompts.

- Look at the rubric on page 49 to review the criteria you will be looking for in assessing your students' writing.

- Read each student's paper. Refer to the rubric to determine which level describes the student's writing. Write the score on the paper.

TIPS FOR WRITING EFFECTIVE LETTERS

1 Think about what you want to say in your letter.

2 Follow the outline on your planning form to write a draft of your letter. For a friendly letter, try to make your letter sound as if you were speaking to the person. Include anecdotes (little stories), descriptions, and details that will make your letter interesting to read.

3 For a business letter, such as a letter of inquiry, be direct and clear. State the subject of your inquiry briefly in the first sentence. Be precise. Instead of asking for all information available, state exactly what you want. Use a separate paragraph for each item requested.

4 Reread what you have written to see if the letter has everything you want to say. Make changes that will improve your letter.

5 Use an editing checklist to help you correct spelling, punctuation, and capitalization. Check to be sure that there is a space between each paragraph or that the first line of each new paragraph has been indented. E-mail has spaces between paragraphs, but the first line of a paragraph is not indented.

6 If you will be sending your letter, recopy your draft.

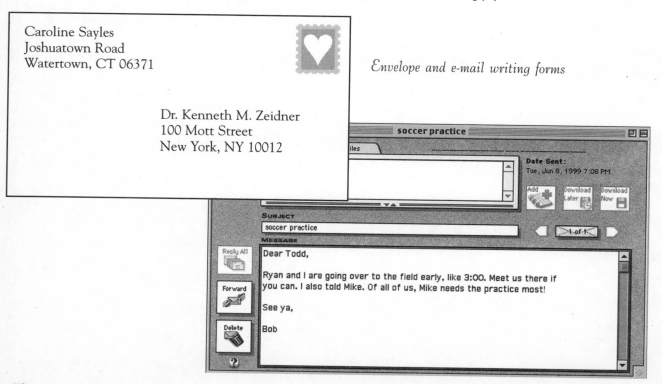

Envelope and e-mail writing forms

Dear Friend...
Planning Form for a Friendly Letter

.... (your address)

.... (city, state, zip)

.... (date)

.... (salutation)

....

....

....

....

....

....

....

....

....

(closing) ....

(your name) ....

Note: Leave an extra space between paragraphs or indent.

Name _____ Date _____

Writing a Friendly Letter

		Yes	**No**
1. The heading shows:			
my address	(line 1)	☐	☐
my city, state, and zip code	(line 2)	☐	☐
the month, date, and year	(line 3)	☐	☐
2. The salutation says "Dear _____," (friend's name)		☐	☐
3. The salutation is followed by a comma.		☐	☐
4. My letter follows the DEAR FRIEND planning outline.		☐	☐
5. The beginning of the letter tells my purpose for writing.		☐	☐
6. My letter includes details, descriptions, and anecdotes that make it interesting to read.		☐	☐
7. I reread what I wrote. It sounds like my own voice.		☐	☐
8. My letter has a satisfying ending.		☐	☐
9. My letter has a closing on the right side of the page (*Sincerely, Love, Your friend*).		☐	☐
10. The closing is followed by a comma.		☐	☐
11. I separated paragraphs.		☐	☐

40 Rubrics & Checklists to Assess Reading and Writing   Scholastic Professional Books

To Whom It May Concern...
Planning Form for a Business Letter

.... (your address)

.... (city, state, zip)

.... (date)

.... (recipient's name)

.... (recipient's address)

.... (city, state, zip)

.... (salutation)

....

....

....

....

....

....

....

....

.... (closing)

.... (your full name)

Note: Leave an extra space between paragraphs.

40 Rubrics & Checklists to Assess Reading and Writing   Scholastic Professional Books

Name _____ Date _____

Writing a Business Letter

	Yes	No
1. Heading #1 has my address, city, state, and zip code	☐	☐
2. Heading #2 has the address, city, state, and zip code of the person who will receive my letter	☐	☐
3. The salutation says "Dear _____," (title and last name of recipient)	☐	☐

....

The body of my letter has:

	Yes	Partly	No
4. an introduction that states my purpose for writing	☐	☐	☐
5. a main section that gives more information	☐	☐	☐
6. an ending statement	☐	☐	☐
7. a closing (*Yours truly*) followed by a comma	☐	☐	☐
8. my signature (first and last names)	☐	☐	☐

....

	Yes	No
9. I have used an editing checklist to correct errors.	☐	☐
10. I separated paragraphs.	☐	☐

40 Rubrics & Checklists to Assess Reading and Writing Scholastic Professional Books

Letter-Writing Rubric

Key Elements and Criteria

◉ **The introduction of a business letter** states the writer's purpose for writing. The letter ends with a closing statement.

◉ **The body of a friendly letter or a business letter** is appropriate for the writer's purpose. A friendly letter is conversational in tone. Anecdotes, descriptions, and details make it interesting to read. The body of a business letter has a clear message that relates to the writer's purpose.

◉ **The format of the letter** follows the planning form guidelines. The heading(s), salutation, and closing are correctly placed and provide the required information.

◉ **The conventions of writing** are followed (capitalization, punctuation, spelling, grammar, and paragraphs).

4	**Proficient**	All four criteria are evident to a high degree.
3	**Capable**	All four criteria are evident. A few errors in format and/or conventions appear.
2	**Satisfactory**	The letter fulfills the writer's purpose. Several errors in format and/or conventions appear.
1	**Beginning**	The letter attempts to fulfill the writer's purpose, but ideas are not adequately developed. There are many errors in format and/or the conventions of writing.

TRY THIS!

STRATEGIES TO BUILD YOUR STUDENTS' LETTER WRITING SKILLS

* Let your students observe you compose a letter using a black felt-tip pen on large chart paper. As you write, point out the placement of the heading, greeting, body, and closing as well as the use of paragraphs, capital letters, and punctuation marks. Display this model on your classroom wall so that students can refer to it when they write their own letters.

* Content-area studies, particularly those which involve students in relevant, real-life inquiries, offer students many opportunities to improve their letter-writing skills. For example, as part of an environmental study, you might ask your students to write letters to invite community experts to your classroom, or to write to the editor of your local newspaper about the importance of recycling waste.

* Most newspapers print letters expressing readers' opinions. Read aloud examples from your local paper and ask your students to write about a community issue that interests them.

* Invite your students to write letters to sports figures. Letters to players on the local team will usually be answered, often with an autographed photo. A paperback listing the mailing addresses of most living major league baseball players can be obtained from Jack Smalling, Baseball Address List, 2308 Van Buren Ave., Ames, IA 50010, for $14.45. Each issue of the magazine Beckett Baseball Card Monthly lists upcoming birthdays of major league baseball players.

* The possibility of getting free or inexpensive products also motivates letter writing. Elizabeth Weiss's book *Free Stuff for Kids* (Meadowbrook, Simon & Schuster, 1992) features over 320 things to write away for.

✸ With the cooperation of another teacher in your own school district or in a different state, you can pair up students to start a pen-pal correspondence.

✸ At the end of the school year, your students could write to students in the grade below theirs with tips on how to be successful in their next grade.

✸ For useful tips on teaching letter writing, see *Putting It in Writing* by Steve Otfinoski (Scholastic, 1993). *Sincerely Yours—How to Write Great Letters* by Elizabeth James and Carol Barkin (Clarion Books, 1993) offers excellent advice to upper elementary students. Also see *Messages in the Mailbox* by Loreen Leedy (Holiday House, 1994).

✸ Encourage your students to use e-mail and other Internet correspondence.

✸ Have your students write thank-you letters to parents and others who have made some contribution or presentation to the class.

✸ At Open House time, tell your students to write letters inviting their family members to visit the school.

Reading Comprehension

Understanding the main characters in a story is often the key to understanding what the story is about. By paying attention to what the characters think and say and how they act toward each other, readers are able to determine what kind of person a character is and see how that character influences the plot. Once upper elementary students have learned how to analyze a single character, they will be able to do the more challenging work of describing the changes in a single character or making character comparisons.

Story problem analysis is another excellent way to determine reading comprehension. By identifying a significant problem in the story and describing the way the main character solves it, students can show us how well they understand the plot and the character. You will find an assessment for analyzing story problems on page 61.

June 16, 1998
Language Arts

Character Sketch - Rudi
Book: Banner in the Sky

Rudi is short for his age of sixteen. His hair is light blond and he has a fair complextion. He is always very polite and curdeous to his elders. Rudi, though he is small, is veryer strong. he is always willing to do something for someone and he tries to help people whenever possible.

Rudi is very selfless because he risked his life to save Saro when he fell from the ridge. Even though he had been mean to Rudi and made it clear to him that he did not like him. In doing so, he gave up the glory and sadisfaction of being the first man to reach the top of the Citadel.

Rudi is also courageous because he took risks. When Captain Winter was trapped in the trench he put his life on the line to try to save him, by taking his own clothes and tying them together. Winter could have pulled him into the trench as well. But he insisted on taking that chance.

Rudi is very much like Robin in The Door in the Wall. They were both very brave and unselfish. Both Rudi and Robin risked their lives to save or help someone else. Rudi saved Captain Winter and Saro. Robin overheard the robbers planning to steal Brother Luke's gold, and woke up John and Luke to warn them. Then, as the robbers were chasing them, he cleverly triped them with his crutch. They were selfless because Rudi risked his life twice to save Saro and Winter, and Robin gave up his time to make poor children toys because he had none.

Example of a sixth grader's character analysis, score 4.

Courtesy of Mrs. R.F. Sandler, sixth grade teacher

Story Character Analysis

✸ Decide whether you will be using the assessment forms for analyzing a main character (pages 55–57) or for analyzing a character's change (pages 58–60).

✸ Select a short story with an interesting and well-developed character. If you plan to have your students analyze a character's change, be sure to find a story that lends itself to that kind of analysis.

✸ Photocopy for each student the short story, the planning form WHAT A CHARACTER! (page 55), and the self-assessment checklist WRITING ABOUT A STORY CHARACTER (page 56). Provide lined paper for rough drafts and final copies of their writing.

✸ Allow plenty of time—at least an hour or an hour and a half—for your students to complete this reading assessment. You may want to use two 45-minute sessions.

PREPARE YOUR STUDENTS

✸ Share the appropriate rubric with your students.

✸ Discuss the meaning of "character traits." Ask your students to suggest traits that are used to describe people, such as *brave, unfriendly, helpful, kind, mean*. Then select one trait—*shy*, for example—and ask them to suggest what a shy person might do at a party.

✸ Distribute copies of WHAT A CHARACTER! and discuss it with your students. Remind them to reread parts of the story to look for specific examples of a character's behavior.

✸ Write the following on a chart or chalkboard.

Good writing should have:
- an interesting introduction
- a main section that gives details and examples to support ideas
- an ending that draws a conclusion about the character
- correct spelling, punctuation, grammar, and paragraphing

If this is a reading assessment, have your students read the story for enjoyment first. Remind them to reread parts of the story to look for specific examples of a character's behavior.

Point out where your students will find the lined paper for their rough drafts and final writing.

Distribute WRITING ABOUT A STORY CHARACTER and suggest that they read the form carefully before they begin to write. Tell them to complete the form after writing their rough drafts and then make any changes that will improve their writing.

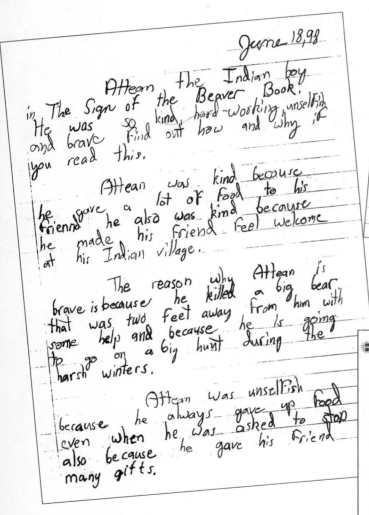

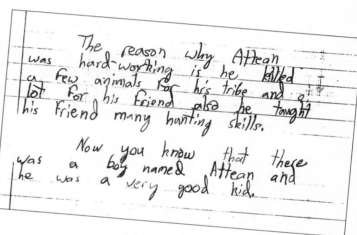

Example of a fourth grader's character analysis (Score 3)

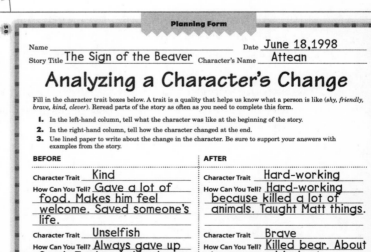

Name _____ Date _____

Story Title _____

Main Character's Name _____

What a Character!

1. Character Trait _____

How Can You Tell? _____

_____

_____

_____

_____

2. Character Trait _____

How Can You Tell? _____

_____

_____

_____

_____

_____

3. Character Trait _____

How Can You Tell? _____

_____

_____

_____

_____

Write about your character on another sheet of paper.

Name _____ Date _____

Story Title _____

Writing About a Story Character

	Yes	No
1. My writing introduced the character in an interesting way.	☐	☐
2. I described the character fully using examples from the story.	☐	☐
3. My ending draws a conclusion about the character.	☐	☐
4. I reread my writing to be sure it was complete.	☐	☐

5. I edited my writing to correct:

	Yes	No
spelling	☐	☐
punctuation	☐	☐
capitalization	☐	☐
grammar	☐	☐
paragraphing	☐	☐
6. I recopied my writing.	☐	☐

40 Rubrics & Checklists to Assess Reading and Writing

Scholastic Professional Books

Rubric for Scoring Writing About a Story Character

4 The written response is fully developed and indicates an excellent understanding of the main character. The traits selected to describe the character are fully supported with accurate, relevant details from the story.

3 The written response indicates a good understanding of the main character. The traits selected to describe the character are adequately supported with accurate, relevant details from the story.

2 The written response is partial and indicates some understanding of the character. Feelings, rather than traits, may be used to describe the character. Opinions and interpretations are minimally supported with details from the story.

1 The response is incomplete. There are few details to support ideas. Or some ideas may indicate a misunderstanding of the character.

Name _____

Date _____

Story Title _____

Character's Name _____

Analyzing a Character's Change

Fill in the character trait boxes below. A trait is a quality that helps us know what a person is like (*shy, friendly, brave, kind, clever*). Reread parts of the story as often as you need to complete this form.

1. In the left-hand column, tell what the character was like at the beginning of the story.

2. In the right-hand column, tell how the character changed at the end.

3. Use lined paper to write about the change in the character. Be sure to support your answers with examples from the story.

BEFORE

Character Trait _____

How Can You Tell? _____
_____
_____

Character Trait _____

How Can You Tell? _____
_____
_____

AFTER

Character Trait _____

How Can You Tell? _____
_____
_____

Character Trait _____

How Can You Tell? _____
_____
_____

40 Rubrics & Checklists to Assess Reading and Writing   Scholastic Professional Books

Name _____ Date _____

Story Title _____

Writing About a Character's Change

	Yes	**No**
1. My writing introduces the character in an interesting way.	☐	☐
2. I use examples from the story to show what the character was like at the beginning.	☐	☐
3. I use examples from the story to show how the character changed. I give reasons for the change.	☐	☐
4. My ending tells what happened as a result of the change.	☐	☐
5. I reread my writing to be sure it was complete.	☐	☐
6. I edited my writing to correct:		
spelling	☐	☐
punctuation	☐	☐
capitalization	☐	☐
grammar	☐	☐
paragraphing	☐	☐
7. I recopied my writing.	☐	☐

40 Rubrics & Checklists to Assess Reading and Writing   Scholastic Professional Books

Rubric for Scoring Writing About a Character's Change

4   The written response is fully developed and indicates an excellent understanding of the character and the change(s) that occurred. Accurate, relevant information selected from the text supports all opinions and interpretations.

3   The response is adequately developed and indicates a fairly good understanding of the character and the change. Some opinions and interpretations are not supported with accurate, relevant evidence from the text.

2   The response is partially developed and indicates some understanding of the character and the change. Many opinions are not supported with accurate or relevant evidence from the text.

1   The response is minimally developed, or inaccurate and irrelevant details and ideas indicate a misunderstanding of the character and the change.

40 Rubrics & Checklists to Assess Reading and Writing

Scholastic Professional Books

Story Problem Analysis

In Advance

⚙ Select a story that you expect most of your students will be able to enjoy. Be sure the story has a main character who has a problem.

⚙ Photocopy the following for each student:

  - the story
  - STORY PROBLEM PLANNING FORM (page 64)
  - WRITING ABOUT A STORY PROBLEM self-assessment checklist (page 65).
  - RUBRIC FOR WRITING ABOUT A STORY PROBLEM (page 66)

TEACHER TIP: If you teach grade 3, you may want to eliminate questions 5 and 6 on the planning form as well as statement #4 on the self-assessment checklist.

⚙ Have lined paper for students to write their responses on.

Prepare Your Students

⚙ Share the rubric on page 66 with your students.

⚙ Discuss the importance of a story problem by saying something like this:

"Every good story—even a fairy tale written long ago—has a problem that the main character faces. Can you describe the story problem in Cinderella? How was the problem resolved? Why do writers create a problem?" (Possible responses: It makes someone want to keep reading to find out how the problem will be solved. You want to find out how the story will end.)

CONDUCT THE ASSESSMENT

✹ Distribute copies of the story.

✹ Distribute the planning form and the self-assessment checklist.

✹ Distribute lined paper.

✹ Read aloud the following information to your students as you point to **each** of the materials you have distributed.

1 Decide what the story problem is.

2 Use the STORY PROBLEM PLANNING FORM to write your ideas.

3 Look at the self-assessment form to see if you need to add examples or information to make your ideas clearer.

4 Write your complete ideas on lined paper. Edit your writing.

5 Complete your self-assessment form. Make any changes that will improve your writing.

Name: Mark Date: 11/15/04

Title and Author: Grandfather's Walking Stick

Write about an important problem in the story. Tell why it is important and how it was solved. by T. Aguallo

The most important problem in this story was that Danny broke his grandfather's walking stick. it was very important to danny's grandfather because the walking stick was only one of it's kind. But Danny tried and tried to think of something to give in return. then he thought of singing a song A song about cowboys. He

sang it once then twice then three times and on the fourth time Danny's grandfather sang along.

Score ❸

◀ *Example of a third grader's analysis of a story problem*

Name JeFF, F   Date 1994

Title and Author Grandfathers Walking stick

Write about an important problem in the story.
Tell why it is important and how it was solved.

The most important
Thing, was that Danny
the little boy told
The truth, Becouse
When he brock the
Stick I bet It
Made danny feel
harrabile. And the
way he made him
feel better. And
I will tell you how
It happened It
all started when

Whos Took grandfathers
walking stick and
slamed it on the
wall.

Score **1**

▲

Example of a third grader's analysis of
a story problem

Name _____ Date _____

Title _____

Story Problem Planning Form

1. The main problem in the story was:

_____
_____
_____

2. The problem was important to the main character because:

_____
_____
_____
_____

3. Attempts to solve the problem (what was tried that did not work) were:

_____
_____
_____

4. The problem was solved when:

_____
_____
_____

5. Think of a different way the problem could have been solved. Be sure that your solution makes sense and is connected to the story's characters and events.

_____
_____
_____

6. How would your solution change the story's ending?

_____
_____
_____

40 Rubrics & Checklists to Assess Reading and Writing Scholastic Professional Books

Name _____ Date _____

Title _____

Writing About a Story Problem

	Yes	No

1. I wrote about an important problem in the story. I told why the problem was important to the main character.

2. I wrote about attempts to solve the problem that did not work. I explained why they did not work.

3. I wrote about how the problem was solved.

4. I described another way the problem could have been solved. My solution is realistic. It connects to the character and events in the story.

5. I reread my writing to be sure it provided accurate, relevant examples and information to support my ideas.

6. I edited my writing to correct:

            spelling

            punctuation

            capitalization

            grammar

            paragraphing

7. I recopied my writing.

Rubric for Writing About a Story Problem

3 The written response is complete. It indicates a very good understanding of the story problem and its resolution. The response provides accurate, relevant examples, information, and supportive reasoning.

2 The response is partial and indicates a fairly good understanding of the story problem and resolution. Although the information selected includes mostly accurate details and ideas, some are irrelevant or unrelated to the story's problem.

1 The written response is partial and indicates some understanding of the character. Feelings, rather than traits, may be used to describe the character. Opinions and interpretations are minimally supported with details from the story.

0 There is little or no response, or inaccurate and irrelevant details and ideas indicate a serious misunderstanding of the story.

40 Rubrics & Checklists to Assess Reading and Writing

Scholastic Professional Books

General Rubric for Story Analysis

3 The writing is fully developed and fulfills all the requirements of the task. It is complete and accurate and indicates a very good understanding of the story and characters. It includes relevant, supportive details and information from the text. Any personal responses are relevant to the task.

2 The writing is adequately developed and fulfills most of the requirements of the task. It provides some relevant, supportive information from the text.

1 The writing includes a few correct details, but ideas may be too general or overly specific. Information about the story may be incomplete.

0 The writing has many inaccuracies and irrelevancies. Equal to a blank paper.

TRY THIS!

STRATEGIES TO BUILD YOUR STUDENTS' STORY AND CHARACTER ANALYSIS SKILLS

🌸 Assemble a collection of articles that will lead students to write a description of the character who owns the items (for example, a soiled T-shirt, a baseball, a news article about baseball, the novel *Catcher with a Glass Arm*). Then have them read aloud and discuss their character analyses in small groups or with the class.

🌸 Discuss the ways authors reveal a character's traits to the reader. (Possible responses include: *the things the character does; what the character says to other characters; the kinds of things the character thinks about; the opinions of other characters.*) Write their responses on a chart.

🌸 Ask your students to write about a character in a novel or short story they are reading. Tell them to list the character's traits and provide evidence from the story that supports their ideas. Remind them to look for evidence in the character's words, thoughts, and actions.

🌸 Show your students how to create a character web that will help them write about a character in a novel or short story. Use the rubric on page 57 to assess their writing.

🌸 Ask your students to compare characters in a novel or short story they have read. Before they write, have them create a web for each character. Then show them how to use Venn diagrams to organize their ideas about the characters' similarities and differences. Use the GENERAL RUBRIC FOR STORY ANALYSIS on page 67 to assess their work.

🌸 Assess your students' listening skills by reading aloud a very short story—such as a fable or folktale—that teaches a lesson. Read the story aloud twice. Before the first reading, tell students to listen carefully so that they can figure out the story's lesson. When you reread the story, have your students take notes about the lesson. Then tell them to write an explanation of the story's lesson. Use the GENERAL RUBRIC FOR STORY ANALYSIS on page 67 to assess their work.

Reading Response Notebooks

Dear Mrs. Weiss,
   The Book I have been reading, "The Loner," I think is boring. I think this because the character is not very strong, the story goes very slowly and it isn't my kind of book. I like comedy, mystery and private criticism books.

                                        from Georgie.

   After reading Georgie's letter, his teacher helped him choose another novel that better matched his interests and reading ability. Then Mrs. Weiss wrote the following response to Georgie in his reading notebook.

Dear Georgie,
   Those are wonderful reasons for changing books. I hope you enjoy "Cracker Jackson." If not, please see me.

                                        Sincerely,
                                        Mrs. Weiss

   This person-to-person form of literary response, developed by Nancie Atwell (1987), encourages students to reflect more thoughtfully on their reading. If your students are already using reading notebooks, you've probably noticed that entries vary in quality. Some will show a reader's thoughtful insights while others are simple summaries (*This story is about…*or *I liked the part when…*). It's important that students be asked to recognize these differences so that they can improve their responses. The rubric on page 80 will help you determine the quality of three responses that your students select as examples of their best thinking.

In Advance

- Make sure all students have a notebook for recording their ideas about the stories they are reading.

- Photocopy the form WHEN I WRITE IN MY READING NOTEBOOK (page 73) for each student.

- Photocopy the self-assessment form MY 3 BEST READING NOTEBOOK ENTRIES (page 74) for each of your students.

- Have on hand several sticky-note pads.

Prepare Your Students

- Allow some time early in the school year—at least three or four weeks—for your students to become accustomed to response writing before making your first assessment.

- Have your students staple the form WHEN I WRITE IN MY READING NOTEBOOK (page 73) inside their notebooks. Explain that they should refer to the form when they're stuck for a writing idea.

- Use some of the TRY THIS! suggestions on page 82 for building your students' response writing skills.

Start With Students' Self-Assessments

- Ask your students to place their reading notebooks on their desks.

- Distribute three sticky notes to each student.

- Show them the rubric (page 80) you will use to assess their entries. Explain the criteria to them.

- Have your students reread their reading responses to find their three best entries. Tell them to tab each of those pages with a sticky note.

- Distribute the self-assessment form MY 3 BEST READING NOTEBOOK ENTRIES. Have your students write their reasons for selecting each entry.

CONDUCT THE ASSESSMENT

◆ Collect the reading notebooks and your students' self-assessment forms.

◆ Use one of the rubrics on pages 80 and 81 to assess the three selected entries. You may also want to refer to your students' self-assessment forms to see what they think is good about each of their selections.

◆ If you want to assess a variety of features in their reading notebooks (for example, development of ideas, originality, readability, or the student's commitment to regular response writing), use the COMPREHENSIVE RUBRIC FOR READING NOTEBOOKS on page 81.

◆ Repeat this assessment at mid-year and in May or June.

AN IMPORTANT NOTE:

As you read your students' entries, focus on the quality of their ideas rather than on writing errors. Since notebook writing is informal, readers usually express their ideas without concern for correctness. (Of course, the writing should be legible enough to communicate meaning.)

Your writing workshop time provides an excellent opportunity for your students to work on improving their use of standard writing conventions. For example, you could ask them to select a "needy" reading log entry, such as the one below, to edit and rewrite using correct grammar, spelling, capitalization, and punctuation.

Nov. 27

Dear Group,

I realy liked this book. When Matt has to make a choys of, if he wants to go with Attean and the trib or stay and wate for his parents. I though that was a prity hard disisoin. I would have done the same thing as Matt did.

◀ *Example of a fourth grader's "needy" log entry about* <u>Sign of the Beaver</u>

English
Section 1

9/19/92

I sometimes ^like to read for pleasure. It depends if it is a good book or not. If it's a enjoyable book I like reading before I go to sleep. If there are good articles about tennis then I'd read those articles. I don't like reading magazines so often. I sometimes talk to my friends about books. I don't have a favorite author. I like a lot of different authors. A book I just read and enjoyed was Alice in Rapture, Sort Of. I don't have any favorite but one of my favorites is probably Deenie. I read it in fifth grade. Deenie because she is funny and makes the book humorous. I usually choose a humor genre when I choose a book. I choose humor genre's because I like reading funny books.

▲

It is also useful to show your students samples of thorough, informative reading log entries to use as models. Above is an example of a sixth grader's proficient reading log entry. (Courtesy of Judy Grosz)

Name _____

When I Write in My Reading Notebook

◎ **I think of interesting ideas and questions to write about.**

I make predictions.

I write my opinion about a book and give reasons for it.

I ask questions about some parts I didn't understand.

I connect what I read to something that happened to me.

I copy a particular line or phrase that I thought was well written.

I compare stories and characters.

I tell why I chose a book or abandoned a book.

I tell about some writing techniques I learned from the author that I want to try in my own stories.

◎ **I show that I understand literary elements (plot, setting, character development, and theme).**

I describe a character's traits (selfish, helpful, shy, friendly, and so on) and give examples from the story that back up my opinions.

I tell how a character changed and give reasons for the change.

I describe the story's problem and its resolution.

I describe the story's setting (where and when it took place).

I write about the story's theme (main idea or author's message).

◎ **I describe the writing styles of authors.**

I tell what I like about the way an author writes.

I compare books by different authors.

I tell which chapter titles I liked and suggest different titles for others.

I copy the author's descriptions that put pictures in my mind (imagery).

I quote lines from a story that show how the author writes.

◎ **I tell about myself as a reader.**

I write about my favorite books and authors.

I describe my childhood memories of stories (favorite titles, being read to, and so on).

I write about an experience I had in a library, book store, or book fair.

I write about the ways I've changed as a reader.

I write about my reading habits—where, when, and how I like to read.

I write about people—family, friends, teachers—who influenced my reading.

Name _____ Date _____

My 3 Best Reading Notebook Entries

🌀 **Date of entry 1:** _____. I think this is one of my best because:

_____

_____

_____

_____

_____

🌀 **Date of entry 2:** _____. I think this is one of my best because:

_____

_____

_____

_____

🌀 **Date of entry 3:** _____. I think this is one of my best because:

_____

_____

_____

_____

_____

40 Rubrics & Checklists to Assess Reading and Writing   Scholastic Professional Books

TIPS FOR ASSESSING READING NOTEBOOK RESPONSES

What you should look for in a notebook entry:

Does the entry demonstrate literary awareness?

For example, does the student:

- describe a story element, such as a character, the plot's problem, the resolution, the setting, or the theme?
- discuss aspects of an author's technique, such as titles, endings, or language?
- criticize or praise something about a book or its author?
- compare and contrast books or authors?

Does the entry describe the student as a reader?

For example, does the student:

- describe her reading processes or preferences?
- discuss changes in book, author, or genre preferences?
- describe informal book discussions with others?
- raise questions, express confusions, or make suggestions?
- give reasons for selecting or abandoning a book?

Is the response complete?

For example, does the student:

- provide sufficient evidence, explanations, reasons, examples, or descriptions to support ideas?

Grade 3, Score ▶

> Dear Dr. F
>
> now at home I am reading <u>Mallory and the trouble with twins</u>. mallory has to babysitt for the Arnold twins. she thinks it will be easy but boy was she wrong. they were running around the house like anamals vas mal relived when ther mother came home I wonder what she will do next.

Dear Dr. F.

when I finish a book it takes me a long time to pick out a nother book. Like I ~~I~~ finished Little Miss Stomeybrook and Dawn a long time ago and I picked out Mary Poppins three days ago. but I chaned books 8 times! ~~I'm reading Stacey says good bye~~ I Like Baby sitter books but my

mother doesn't because first they ~~a~~ talk about the peopl who they babby sitt an stuff Like that.

Take a look at this literary letter featuring a reflection on Roald Dahl's writing style. How does it measure on the literary awareness scale? ▶

Dear Dr. Fiderer.   2/11

Roald Dahl's stories are njoyed by all children because he very well knew what child loved. He wrote stories about love, suspense, action, ghosts, finding treasure, choclates, toys, magic an money because he knew children would love them. He wrote stories which made children giggle. He thought that writing for kids w~~r~~ harder because they don't have concentration as adults do, so he wrote in such a way that they would hold the story fr~~u~~ the start to end. The life of a writer really suited him very well, because he had no boss except his own soul.

The Hoopples Horrible Holiday

I think this book is good so far because its funny. I think the Hoopples will go to there grandmothers house and sit down to eat and something will go wrong. I choose this book because the cover looked funny and the title was good. I also choose it because I like to read the authours books so far I have read two of his books Chicken Trek and the Oscar J noodleman telivision network.

◀ **Grade 4, Score ❸**

In her entry, this student makes inferences about the plot; describes her book-selection process, and names other works by the same author.

Grade 4, Score ❷ ▶

Dear Dr. Fiderer,
The book I'm reading now Is a very good book. It is about a dog, cat and rabbit and John and Hata have read to. They find the rabbit when one of the boys sits on something. The family has a mom, dad,

PS: Guess What book it is.

1/28/91

Dear Dr Fiderer,
I am reading The Celery Stalks At Midnight.
It has been a reel adventer so I realy
want to get back to the book. Bunnicik is
lost now and everybody is going to look for him.
I think he's just hinding somewhere.

◄ **Grade 4, Score** **1**

Grade 4, Score **0** ►

Oct. 16, 1990

Dear Dr Fiderer,
the book i was
reading and atlast
i finished the book.

May 14, 1993

Dear Mrs Weiss
Sing Down The Moon had a lot of
detail and desruption. Like when the
boys grandfather came back
to life after being dead for a
while. I this book white men
treated the Indians like they
were animals. One of the main
chartors a Indian named Tall
Boy he was shot by Spaniards
I thought that was the worst
part of the book. I would
recomend this book to Brian because
he would love it and he usually
reads books that I read.

◄ **Grade 5, Score** **3**

This student identifies an
important theme in the story
and shows he is aware of his
own and his friend's literary
preferences.

She appreciates the
drama of the storyline.

I am reading Hari's
Blood it is a very
good book to read aloud
with expression which I do
at home!

I saw a cartoon about
two or three weeks ago
it was on C.B.S which
always have a cartoon
a-bout a book once a
week every Saturday.

She compares the book
to a cartoon version
and provides an example
to explain her opinion.

And I saw the cartoon
of Hari's Blood a Saturday
which was only for a
half an Hour.

I just can't believe
it. A half Hour cartoon.
And this Book takes
about 3 weeks to read!!

I guess its just like
this part in the book:

Here she shows an appreciation
for the imagery in the
language of the text.

"The second moon
had just lipped the
horizon when Jakkin
checked the barn again."

That just shows a
picture in the cartoon.

◀ Grade 5, Score ④

Grade 6, Score ③ ▶

9/19/92

English
Section 1

                    like
I sometimes ∧ to read for pleasure
it depends if it's a good
book or not. If it's a enjoyable
book I like reading before I
go to sleep. If there are good
articles about tennis then
I'd read those articles. I don't
like reading magazines so
often. I sometimes talk to
my friends about books. I
don't have a favorite author.
I like a lot of different
authors. A book I just read and
enjoyed was Alice in Rapture, Sort
Of. I don't have any favorite
but one of my favorites is probably
Deenie. I read it in fifth grade.
Deenie because she is funny
and makes the book humorous. I
usually choose a humor genre when
I choose a book. I choose humor
genre's because I like reading funny books.

Rubric for Assessing Reading Notebook Responses

4 The response indicates an excellent understanding of the story. All ideas are fully supported with evidence (quotes) from the text, explanations, interpretations, or examples. A response may describe the student's strong interest in books and reading.

3 The response indicates a good understanding of the story. Ideas are supported with adequate evidence from the text, explanations, or reasons. A response may show questions raised and answered by the student, or it may provide evidence of the student's interest in books and reading.

2 An opinion followed by a brief, relevant summary or reaction with few or no explanations indicates that the student has read the story (*I liked the part where....I was surprised when...*).
A response may pose a question the student has about the story, or it may provide evidence of the student's reading processes and preferences.

1 The response is brief and indicates a minimal understanding of the story. Ideas and opinions are not supported with evidence.

0 Inaccurate and irrelevant details indicate a serious misunderstanding of stories, or there is not sufficient information to make an assessment.

40 Rubrics & Checklists to Assess Reading and Writing Scholastic Professional Books

Comprehensive Rubric for Reading Notebooks

KEY ELEMENTS	CRITERIA		
	3 Excellent	**2** Satisfactory	**1** Needs Improvement
Development of response ideas	Most opinions and ideas are fully supported with explanations and evidence.	Many opinions and ideas are supported with details.	Few ideas are developed.
Commitment to writing responses independently from mid-September to mid-June	25 or more entries	18–24 entries	17 or fewer
Original and interesting ideas	Many entries	Some entries	Few entries
Readability: legible writing; titles are capitalized and underlined.	Most entries	Many entries	Some entries

TRY THIS!

STRATEGIES TO BUILD THOUGHTFUL LITERARY RESPONSES

- Make a chart or photocopy a sheet of sentence stems that your students can use to begin a log entry, such as: *I noticed…I was surprised…I wonder why…This chapter was mainly about…This story reminds me of…I predict that…I think…If I were…I'm not sure…My favorite…I can't really understand…I like the way…I wish…*

- Ask your students to use sticky notes to capture their "in-the-moment" thoughts and reactions to a story while they are reading. Suggest that they refer to these notes to write their log entries.

- Model a literary response by reading aloud your own "sticky-note" notes about a story you are reading. Then verbally demonstrate how you would more fully develop the brief notes for a response-log entry.

- As a prewriting strategy, show your students how to use graphic organizers such as Venn diagrams, webs, or story maps to help them generate and organize their ideas. See *Literacy Through Literature* by Terry Johnson and Daphne Lewis (Heinemann, 1988) for creative examples of literary graphic organizers.

- Read a story chapter aloud, then hold a discussion.

- Have your students edit and recopy their favorite reading log responses for a bulletin board display or for inclusion in their "best work" portfolios.

- Once every few weeks have your students select an interesting log entry to read to a partner or small group.

- Collect each student's reading log periodically and write a response to one entry. You'll find helpful tips for managing this dialogue process, as well as examples of teachers' comments, in *In the Middle: Writing, Reading, and Learning With Adolescents* by Nancie Atwell (Boynton/Cook, 1998).

- Periodically, pair up your students to exchange literary letters about the books they're reading. Remind them to use the rubric on page 49 to guide their letter writing. Then have them write a response to their partner's letter using the rubric to provide feedback.

- Create your own rubric to assess your students' diligence in writing regularly in their response notebooks. For example: Overall, the number of responses in the notebook indicates a commitment to regular response writing:

3 Strongly   **2** Adequately   **1** Minimally

Reading Record Assessments

I t's important for us to keep track of our students' reading patterns and preferences, such as the titles and genres they select for independent reading. We also need to assess, or have our students assess, the contributions they make in their small-group book discussions or what they say and do when they give a book presentation to tell their classmates about a novel they have read. But assessing each of these important reading-related components takes time! The best solution I have found is to let my students keep their own records and make some of the rubric assessments for me.

IN ADVANCE

- Provide, or have your students make, record forms for recording book titles, book genres, novel group discussions, book presentations, or any other reading-related activity you would like to have them assess.

- Photocopy one of the rubrics on pages 84–86 for each of your students.

- Plan to allow several minutes or so at the end of an activity for your students to complete the rubric assessment.

PREPARE YOUR STUDENTS

- Explain that you've come up with an idea that will help you keep track of their various reading time activities, then show your students the rubric and ask them to suggest any criteria that could be added or revised.

CONDUCT THE ASSESSMENT

- Have students place on their desks the rubric you have selected and, if appropriate, any record forms, such as book lists.

Name _____ Date _____

Student's Rubric for Assessing Book Lists

Criteria	**3** Consistently	**2** Most of the time	**1** Sometimes
I recorded all book titles and authors' names.			
I wrote the dates I started and completed each book.			
I used the conventions of writing (capitalization, spelling, punctuation).			

Analyze Your Book List

1. Study your book list and make notes about:

a. the number of books you've read and why you've read so many or so few

_____

_____

b. their level of reading challenge (challenging, medium, easy)

_____

_____

c. your favorite author and why you like that author

_____

_____

d. your favorite series and why you like it

_____

_____

e. any changes you notice from September to the present

_____

_____

40 Rubrics & Checklists to Assess Reading and Writing Scholastic Professional Books

Student's Rubric for Assessing Book Group Discussions

Note to the teacher:

1. Make a photocopy of this rubric for each group. Discuss the criteria with your students.

2. After a book discussion, have the group members determine their group's score for each of the criteria. Ask one student in each group to record the score.

Key Elements	❸ Excellent	❷ Satisfactory	❶ Needs Improvement
Level of Participation	Each member was equally involved in the discussions.	Most were involved.	Few were involved. One or two did most of the talking.

Write your group's score here: _____

Listening	Each member made eye contact with the speaker. No one distracted the group.	Most members paid attention to the speaker.	Few paid attention to the speaker.

Write your group's score here: _____

On-task Behavior	Discussion was on the topic for the entire time.	There was some off-topic behavior, but members got one another right back on task.	Much off-task behavior. Teacher had to help.

Write your group's score here: _____

Preparation	Each member was fully prepared for the discussion.	Most members were fully prepared for the discussion.	Few members were prepared for the discussion.

Write your group's score here: _____

Title of book: _____ Date _____

Names of group members: _____

Name of student recorder: _____

Student's Rubric for Assessing Book Presentations

Note to the teacher:

◉ Before using the following rubric, provide a sign-up list on a chart or chalkboard so that three or four students can sign up each day to make individual five-minute book presentations to the class. Discuss the purpose of book presentations: *Tell just enough about the plot, the characters, and the theme (the author's message) to make others want to read your book and find out how it ends. Give evidence from the story to back up your statements and opinions.*

◉ Show your students the rubric. Answer their questions.

◉ After a student's presentation, in a one-to-one conference, use the rubric to point out what the student could do to improve the next presentation.

◉ Provide photocopies of the rubric so that students can assess each other's presentations.

Key Elements	**3** Excellent	**2** Satisfactory	**1** Needs Improvement
Content	Discusses main ideas, theme, plot and characters; supports opinions with evidence from the story; organizes ideas well.	Describes events and characters, and gives opinions.	Tells a little about a character or an event; rates the books [*good, boring*] with no explanations.
Presentation Skills	Speaks clearly and audibly all of the time.	Speaks clearly and audibly most of the time.	Speaks audibly some of the time.
Presentation Stance	Stands erect; maintains eye contact with audience.	Stands erect and makes eye contact most of the time.	Fidgets; rarely stands erect or makes eye contact.

40 Rubrics & Checklists to Assess Reading and Writing

Scholastic Professional Books

TRY THIS!

STRATEGIES TO IMPROVE GROUP BOOK DISCUSSIONS AND INDIVIDUAL BOOK PRESENTATIONS

* Have your students refer to WHEN I WRITE IN MY READING NOTEBOOK on page 73 to help them find ideas for their discussions and book presentations.

* Have a student make a storyboard by drawing four to six important scenes from the book on unlined sheets of paper. Create a transparency of the storyboard and project it on an overhead screen for a book presentation.

* Plan mini-lessons that will help students better understand and communicate the elements of stories, such as setting, mood, and point of view.

* Have each group member prepare three or four questions to get a discussion started. You may want to give each one a list of question starters to help them write their questions. For example: *How come…? Why do you think…? If you were the author…? How is this book like (or different from) another you've read? How are you like (or different from) (name of a story character)? Has anyone you know ever…? If you were (character), what would you have done? Does this story remind you of something that happened to you…or of another story you've read?*

* As your students read, tell them to use sticky notes for tabbing the pages that they'd like to discuss with their group members.

* Help your students develop a chart of discussion guidelines. For example:

    1 Write your questions or ideas before coming to a meeting.

    2 Respond to your group members' questions and ideas.

    3 If you disagree with someone's opinion, offer your own idea. Be sure to give evidence from the story that supports your opinion.

    4 Predict what might happen next in the story.

Content-Area Research

I f you are like most elementary teachers, you know how important it is to integrate your science and social studies subjects with reading and writing. Through their research studies, your students probably create posters, dioramas, models, booklets, hypertext compositions, speeches, informational picturebooks, and play scripts. These variations on the traditional written report are dynamic ways for kids to show what they know, but assessing these creative efforts can pose a challenge.

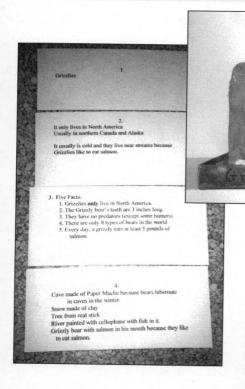

Grizzlies   1

2.
It only lives in North America.
Usually in northern Canada and Alaska

It usually is cold and they live near streams because
Grizzlies like to eat salmon.

3. Five Facts:
   1. Grizzlies **only** live in North America.
   2. The Grizzly bear's teeth are 3 inches long.
   3. They have no predators (except some hunters)
   4. There are only 8 types of bears in the world
   5. Every day, a grizzly eats at least 5 pounds of
      salmon.

4.
Cave made of Paper Mache because bears hibernate
   in caves in the winter.
Snow made of clay
Tree from real stick
River painted with cellophane with fish in it.
Grizzly bear with salmon in his mouth because they like
   to eat salmon.

Photographs and writing samples of content-area research and presentations. You should notice that they represent a variety of proficiency levels. If you were scoring these pieces of work, how would they rate on your rubric?

Otherwise Known as the
Aquatic Moth Caterpillar

With the naked eye it looks like a gray creature swimming around very fast in the water, but look at it though a microscope it is green and white. Those are the ways I looked at the Aquatic Moth Caterpillar. It is also called the Lily-Leaf Caterpillar.

It is about an inch long. It eats leaves, but I think it mainly eats lilypads which is a form of leaves.

Most of them resemble caddisworms with the way they lead their lives. For example, they both eat leaves. The lily-leaf caterpillar has thread-like gills otherwise they look mainly like a typical caterpillar. There is another type that has no gills but breathes from a bubble trapped in its case.

Try your hand at scoring the science reports on this page and the following. If necessary, use a plus or minus to help score the writing.

By taking a lilyleaf and cutting two pieces each around a inch long and stitching it together with silk it makes a shelter.

The common lily-leaf caterpillar lives in a lily pad pond where the water is calm.

The next time I go to a lily-pad pond I'll try and catch *one*.

READING COMPREHENSION SCORE 3
WRITING EFFECTIVENESS SCORE _____

RUBRIC FOR ASSESSING RESEARCH REPORT WRITING (INDIVIDUAL)

SUBJECT/TOPIC *Aquatic Moth Caterpillar*

	LEVEL 3	LEVEL 2	LEVEL 1
Comprehension of Subject/topic:	Writing indicates an excellent understanding of the topic. Reflects use of a range of resources.	Writing indicates a satisfactory understanding of the topic. Reflects the use of one or more resources.	Writing indicates a limited understanding of the topic. Contains factual errors and may be missing critical information.
Writing Effectiveness:			
Idea Development	Develops relevant ideas clearly and fully. Information focuses on the topic. Details, examples, anecdotes, or personal experiences explain and clarify the information.	Develops ideas satisfactorily with adequate details, examples, anecdotes, or experiences.	Develops ideas incompletely with few or no supporting details. Some information may be unrelated to the topic.
Organization	Organizes information logically in paragraphs. Includes an effective introduction and ending that engage the reader.	Organizes information in an an acceptable order that is easy to understand. Paragraphs may be used inconsistently.	Presents ideas with little or no organization.
Language Usage	Uses lively and descriptive language. Details, anecdotes, and examples explain and clarify information. Varies sentence length and structure.	Uses some descriptive language. Demonstrates some sense of sentence variety.	Uses limited vocabulary. Uses repetitive, simple sentences.
Mechanics	Writing shows few errors in basic language conventions.	Limited errors in basic language conventions do not interfere with meaning.	Shows many errors in conventions, but still conveys some meaning.

A zero paper has many factual errors, or is so unclear that the reader cannot understand what is written.

Unicorn of the Sea

A Unicorn is an imaginary animal. Can you believe that the Narwhal is like a Unicorn? Well, you had better believe it! Because that's what this chapter is about!

The Narwhal is a very different kind of whale. Many people think the Narwhal is dangerous and a tormentor. But if you knew that the species is a close relative of the Beluga, you wouldn't be so doubtful.

Many whalers hunt this mammal for its ivory tusk. The tusk is really the Narwhal's only tooth. It sticks out of the upper jaw like a titanic horn. Only the male has the tusk. The female has several jagged teeth on the side of the mouth. A Narwhal's tusk can pierce an enemy's skin. Naturalists and scientists are still baffled with its characteristics; The deep set pectoral fin, the dark spots, and the sensitive eyes. But the most enigmatic puzzle is the blowhole! Whales have two nostrils but dolphins have but one hole on the top of the head. Whales have nostrils, right? Right! And Dolphins have one blowhole, right? Right! The Narwhal is a whale, right? Right! So why does the Narwhal have one blowhole and not two nostrils? Don't be upset because you can't answer that question... Scientists have been trying for thirty years!

Adult Narwhals are almost white in color, but new-born Narwhals are almost black.

The Narwhal's worst enemy is the bull shark. You see the migration pattern of the Narwhal is the same as the Bull shark's.

Speaking of the Narwhal, how would you like to go through life with a long hood-ornament mounted on your skull?!

COMPREHENSION SCORE _3_

WRITING EFFECTIVENESS SCORE _____

RUBRIC FOR ASSESSING RESEARCH REPORT WRITING

SUBJECT/TOPIC _Whales_

	LEVEL 3	LEVEL 2	LEVEL 1
Comprehension of Subject/topic:	Writing indicates an excellent understanding of the topic. Reflects use of a range of resources.	Writing indicates a satisfactory understanding of the topic. Reflects the use of one or more resources.	Writing indicates a limited understanding of the topic. Contains factual errors and may be missing critical information.
Writing Effectiveness:			
Idea Development	Develops relevant ideas clearly and fully. Information focuses on the topic. Details, examples, anecdotes, or personal experiences explain and clarify the information.	Develops ideas satisfactorily with adequate details, examples, anecdotes, or experiences.	Develops ideas incompletely with few or no supporting details. Some information may be unrelated to the topic.
Organization	Organizes information logically in paragraphs. Includes an effective introduction and ending that engage the reader.	Organizes information in an acceptable order that is easy to understand. Paragraphs may be used inconsistently.	Presents ideas with little or no organization.
Language Usage	Uses lively and descriptive language. Details, anecdotes, and examples explain and clarify information. Varies sentence length and structure.	Uses some descriptive language. Demonstrates some sense of sentence variety.	Uses limited vocabulary. Uses repetitive, simple sentences.
Mechanics	Writing shows few errors in basic language conventions.	Limited errors in basic language conventions do not interfere with meaning.	Shows many errors in conventions, but still conveys some meaning.

A zero paper has many factual errors, or is so unclear that the reader cannot understand what is written.

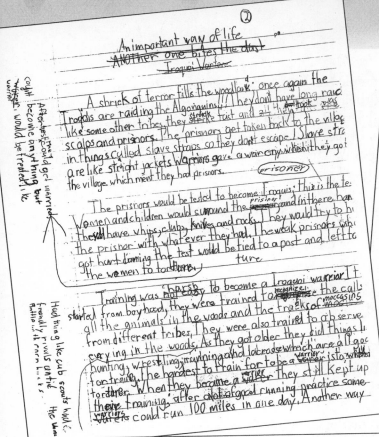

An Important Way of Life

A shriek of terror fills the woodlands; once again the Iroquois are raiding the Alganquins!!! They don't have long raids like some other tribes, they struck fast and they took scalps and prisnors. The prisnors get taken back to the village in things called slave straps so they don't escape. Slave straps are like straight jackets. Warriors gave a war cry when they got to the village which ment they had prisoners.

The prisnors would be tested to become Iroquois. This is the test. Women and children would surround the prisnor, and in there hand they would have whips, clubes, knives and rocks. They would try to hit the prisnor with whatever they had. The weak prisnors who got hurt during the test would be tied to a post left to the women to torture. After the test they could get married. They couldn't become anything but would be treated like warriors.

Training was harsh to become a Iroquoi warrior. It started from boyhood, they were trained to recognize the call all the animals in the woods and the tracks of moccasins from different tribes. They were also trained to observe everything in the woods. As they got older they did things like hunting, wrestling, running and lacrosse which are all good for training. The hardest thing to train for to be a warrior is to kill and torturer. When they became a warrior they still kept up their training; after a lot of good running practice some warriors could run 100 miles in one day.

Another way Iroquis boys were trained was a group of boys would gather with a wise man of the village. This is what he'd tell the boys to do.

"Gather at the council rock (the meeting rock) down by the river. There take of all your clothes and run to the trail house (an open camp provided for travelers). Stay there until you make a fire. gather materials for clothing, kill a dear or beaver, make a pair of moccasins and bring back enough fishes for the house of the Wolf. If you don't I'll send the Black bear band after you with weapons and they will kill you."

If it took the boy too long, the answer would be "Try again." This would go on until the boy learned to do this fast enough.

The Iroquis were very searious about warfare; it was one of their most important ways of life.

Drafting, conferring, revising: the keys to improving report writing

The preceding examples highlight the diversity of styles students can choose to report their information as well as the varying degrees of quality in the final products. How do we define just what makes a particular report, poster, or diorama excellent, good, or not-so-good? Rubrics can show us the way. These excellent tools establish descriptions of various performance levels and allow us to assess our students' research efforts as well as their reports, projects, and presentations. In this section you'll find samples of rubrics for research reports, informational picture books, and dioramas. You can use one of the general rubrics on pages 105 and 106 for assessing your own content-area project.

In Advance

✸ Make photocopies of the RESEARCH READING LOG form on page 96 so that your students can list the books they read to learn about their subject.

✸ Gather plenty of informational resources on the main topic your class will study, including trade books, magazine articles, and textbooks as well as non-print materials such as videos, photographs, and CD-ROMs.

✸ Provide, or ask students to obtain, 5″ X 8″ index cards.

A Research/Writing Assessment

Prepare Your Students

✸ Show your students the rubric you plan to use to assess their work.

✸ Help your students select a manageable, limited topic for their research reports. One good way is to show your students how to use a graphic organizer such as the "Bubble Outline" on page 93. Then have them create another bubble outline for their own report.

✸ Have your students write the subtopics as headings on separate index cards. After reading to find information, tell them to record what they have learned on the appropriate cards.

✸ Allow plenty of time—at least three weeks—for reading, drafting, conferring, editing, and rewriting their reports.

CONDUCT THE ASSESSMENT

✹ Before they begin to write their reports, show your students the RESEARCH REPORT WRITING CHECKLIST on page 98 and review the criteria with them. After completing their reports the students should use the same checklist to rate their work.

✹ Collect your students' RESEARCH READING LOGS, research reports, and self-assessment checklists.

✹ Use the rubric on page 99 to assess their research reports.

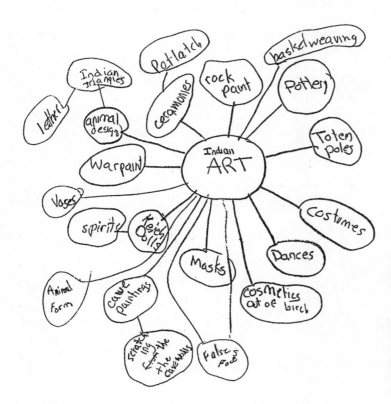

▲
Example of a student's graphic organizer for selecting a manageable writing topic

A Research Project and Presentation Assessment

TEACHER TIP

It will make your assessments easier at the beginning if you assign one type of project for the entire class (for example, a diorama, an informational booklet, a model, or a poster). Assessing similar types of projects will make it easier for you to see differences in achievement. There are also instructional benefits. Since all students will be working on the same format, your lessons and resource materials will be relevant to every project.

IN ADVANCE

- Prepare enough drawing paper for all students to sketch a plan for their project.

- Photocopy the general rubric on page 105 to assess your students' projects. You can easily customize this rubric by adding criteria relevant to a specific topic.

PREPARE YOUR STUDENTS

- Share with your students the general rubric on page 105.

- Have your students review their research information to find an idea for a project.

- Distribute blank sheets of paper for your students to sketch their ideas of what their project will look like. Explain that a sketch is a plan and should include a drawing as well as labels for different parts of the drawing.

- Have your students list the materials they will use for their projects (for example, shallow boxes for dioramas, construction paper, plasticene clay, and cardboard).

⚬ If your students will be working in groups, show them how to divide the project into small, well-defined tasks. (See, for example, the group planning form on page 102 for making an informational picture book.)

⚬ Plan to give the same score to each member of a cooperative group. You can explain this by pointing out that group work is similar to teamwork in a football or baseball game where there is a single final score for everyone on the team.

CONDUCT THE ASSESSMENT

⚬ Distribute copies of the RESEARCH AND PROJECT CHECKLIST on page 97. Tell your students they will need to examine their RESEARCH READING LOGS, research cards, and projects before completing this checklist.

⚬ Have your students give oral presentations to explain their projects. Select an appropriate oral presentation rubric from pages 101 and 104, or use one of the blank rubric forms at the end of this book to create your own. Refer to the rubric while listening to a presentation so that you can make an immediate assessment. Encourage questions from the audience.

⚬ Use the rubrics on pages 101 and 103 to assess informational books and dioramas. Use one of the general rubrics on pages 105 and 106 for assessing other projects and presentations.

Name _____ Date _____

Research Topic _____

Research Reading Log

(Title of Book)   (Author)

_____

_____

_____

_____

_____

_____

_____

_____

The book that gave me the most interesting information on my topic was:

_____

For example, I learned: _____

_____

_____

_____

40 Rubrics & Checklists to Assess Reading and Writing

Scholastic Professional Books

Name _____ Date _____

Research Topic _____

Research and Project Checklist

1 My Reading Log shows that I read _____ books to learn about my topic. The following book or books taught me a lot about my topic:

_____

_____

2 My research cards show that I learned about: (List at least 4 subtopics)

a. _____

b. _____

c. _____

d. _____

e. _____

3 My project shows:

_____

_____

_____

4 On a scale of 1–5, I would rate my project a _____ because:

_____

_____

Name _____ Date _____

Research Topic _____

Research Report Writing Checklist

My writing shows that:

	Yes	Partly	No
1. I understand my topic. I used books and other resources (e.g., video, CD-ROM) to get information.	☐	☐	☐
2. I wrote an interesting introduction for my topic.	☐	☐	☐
3. I develop my ideas clearly with explanations, details, and examples.	☐	☐	☐
4. I organize my information in paragraphs. I indent the first line of a new paragraph.	☐	☐	☐
5. I use descriptive language, strong verbs, and specific nouns.	☐	☐	☐
6. I know how to use writing conventions such as:			
capital letters	☐	☐	☐
punctuation	☐	☐	☐
correct spellings	☐	☐	☐
7. I know how to write a complete sentence.	☐	☐	☐
8. I can write an ending that sums up my ideas.	☐	☐	☐
9. I made a bibliography that lists the books I read.	☐	☐	☐

10. I think this report is (well done, average, in need of improvement) because:

_____

_____

40 Rubrics & Checklists to Assess Reading and Writing

Scholastic Professional Books

Subject/Topic _____

Rubric for Research Report Writing

Key Elements	Evaluative Criteria
Comprehension of Subject/Topic	The writing indicates a complete understanding of the topic and reflects the use of a range of resources. The bibliography lists a variety of sources (for example, nonfiction texts, print and electronic articles, and audiovisual resources).

Writing Effectiveness:

Idea Development	The writer develops relevant ideas clearly and fully. Information focuses on the topic. Details, examples, anecdotes, or personal experiences explain and clarify the information.
Organization	The writer organizes information logically in paragraphs. Includes an effective introduction and ending that engages the reader.
Language Usage	The writer provides lively and descriptive language. Details, anecdotes, and examples explain and clarify information.
Mechanics	Writing shows few errors in basic language conventions.

Scoring Levels

Comprehension of Subject/Topic:

3 Excellent

2 Satisfactory

1 Somewhat evident

Writing Effectiveness:

All four key elements are evident:

3 to a high degree

2 to a satisfactory degree

1 to a limited degree

0 No key elements are adequately demonstrated; equal to a blank paper.

Name _____

Rubric for Assessing Research Report Writing

Subject/Topic: _____

_____ Reading Comprehension Score   _____ Writing Effectiveness Score

	Level  3	Level 2	Level 1
Comprehension of Subject/Topic	Writing indicates an excellent understanding of the topic. Reflects use of a range of resources.	Writing indicates a satisfactory understanding of the topic. Reflects the use of one or more resources.	Writing indicates a limited understanding of the topic. Contains factual errors and may be missing critical information.
Writing Effectiveness:			
Idea Development	Develops relevant ideas clearly and fully. Information focuses on the topic. Details, examples, anecdotes, or personal experiences explain and clarify the information.	Develops ideas satisfactorily with adequate details, examples, anecdotes, or experiences.	Develops ideas incompletely with few or no supporting details. Some information may be unrelated to the topic. Information may be copied from a book without attribution.
Organization	Organizes information logically in paragraphs. Includes an effective introduction and ending that engage the reader.	Organizes information in an acceptable order that is easy to understand. Paragraphs may be used inconsistently.	Presents ideas with little or no organization.
Language Usage	Uses lively and descriptive language. Deatils, anecdotes, and examples explain and clarify information. Varies sentence structure.	Uses some descriptive language. Demonstrates some sense of sentence variety.	Uses limited vocabulary. Uses repetitive, simple sentences.
Mechanics	Writing shows few errors in basic language conventions.	Limited errors in basic language conventions do not interfere with meaning.	Shows many errors in conventions, but still conveys some meaning.

A zero paper has many factual errors, or is so unclear that the reader cannot understand what is written.

Adapted from a rubric developed by fourth grade teachers in Quaker Ridge Elementary School. The rubric uses scoring criteria from the New York State English Language Arts Assessment.

Rubric for Assessing Dioramas and Projects

③ Capable

The diorama is carefully constructed, visually appealing, and three-dimensional. The background drawing and standing cutouts and figures convey important information about the subject (e.g., appearance, food, and shelter) and its environment. Display cards provide interesting facts related to elements displayed in the diorama or to the topic.

② Satisfactory

The diorama displays relevant details about the subject and its environment. The information is presented through the background drawings pasted inside the box and a few standing cutouts or toy figures. Display cards provide some additional information about elements shown in the diorama.

① Beginning

A drawing (e.g., trees or sky) pasted onto the back of the diorama includes few details about the subject or its environment. Or: drawings and cutouts are not constructed well enough to convey information. Display cards provide a label but few facts about the subject and/or its environment.

Oral Presentation of the Diorama's Subject and Its Environment

④ Indicates an excellent understanding.

③ Indicates an adequate understanding.

② Includes some accurate information. Some facts may be inaccurate.

① Provides few facts. Some comments may be inaccurate or irrelevant.

Group _____ Date _____

Group Work Plan for an Informational Picture Book

This book will be mainly about _____.

The book will be written and illustrated by (names of group members):

_____

The book's title will be _____.

Our book will tell about _____

_____.

Our Plan for the Book's Pages

Topics	Writer	Artist
1. _____		
2. _____		
3. _____		
4. _____		
5. _____		
6. _____		

The book's cover will be made by _____.

The Table of Contents will be made by _____.

List any additional sections on the back (Title Page, Glossary, Subject Index, and Bibliography) and tell who will make them.

40 Rubrics & Checklists to Assess Reading and Writing Scholastic Professional Books

Rubric for Informational Picture Books

Key Elements

◎ Quality of information provided by the text

◎ Quality and relevance of information conveyed by the illustrations

◎ Degree of care given to the book's construction

◎ Quality of the Table of Contents and Bibliography

Criteria/Score

4
- The text consistently provides important, accurate information.
- All illustrations fully support the text and may include details that convey additional information.
- The book was constructed with care. The artwork on the book's cover and pages is visually appealing and displays accurate details about the subject.
- Most of the text follows the conventions of writing.
- The Table of Contents and Bibliography are complete.

3
- The text usually provides important, accurate information about the subject. Some irrelevant information may appear.
- Most illustrations support the information in the text.
- Many parts of the book were constructed with care. Several errors in writing conventions appear.
- The Table of Contents or the Bibliography may be incomplete.

2
- The text may provide partial information, or some information is inaccurate or irrelevant.
- Some illustrations do not support the information in the text.
- Some parts of the book were constructed with care.
- The Table of Contents and/or the Bibliography may be incomplete.

1
- Much information is inaccurate or irrelevant.
- Many illustrations do not support the information in the text.
- Few parts of the book are constructed with care.
- The Table of Contents or the Bibliography is missing.

Rubric for Project Presentations

Key elements of an excellent presentation:

◎ Provides accurate details and explanations about elements in the project.

◎ Explains how the project is related to the main research topic.

◎ Answers questions knowledgeably.

◎ Speaks clearly and audibly.

4	**Proficient**	All four key elements are demonstrated to a high degree.
3	**Capable**	All four key elements are adequately demonstrated.
2	**Satisfactory**	Three key elements are adequately demonstrated.
1	**Developing**	Two key elements are adequately demonstrated.

40 Rubrics & Checklists to Assess Reading and Writing Scholastic Professional Books

Rubric for Various Projects and Presentations

Criteria/Key Elements

⊚ **Quality of Ideas**

(The project teaches others important information about the topic in a creative way. Descriptive labels or signs provide details about the subject.)

⊚ **Care and Creativity**

(The project is well constructed and visually appealing.)

⊚ **Presentation**

(The oral presentation provides relevant information not evident in the project alone and reflects the use of various resources.)

Scoring Guide

3 All key elements are evident to a high degree.

2 All key elements are evident.

1 Few key elements are evident to a satisfactory degree.

General Rubric for Reading, Research Notes, and Presentations

Evaluative Criteria/Key Elements

....

◎ **Reading Log** lists several sources for information.

◎ **Research Note Cards** provide accurate information about the subject and reflect the use of a variety of resources.

◎ **Presentation** provides accurate, complete, and relevant information on the topic and answers questions posed by classmates and teacher.

4	**Proficient**	All three criteria are evident to a high degree.
3	**Capable**	All three criteria are evident to a high or moderate degree.
2	**Satisfactory**	All criteria are evident to a moderate degree.
1	**Beginning**	Few criteria are evident.

TRY THIS!

STRATEGIES TO IMPROVE YOUR STUDENTS' RESEARCH REPORTS

* Limit their writing topics. Have your students select specific, individual topics on the broad subject the class is studying.

* Demonstrate note-taking strategies such as writing important ideas that tell about the topic, keeping notes short, and organizing notecards by topic.

* To discourage copying information from texts word for word, show your students how you use your own words to rephrase information in a paragraph. Also demonstrate the way you place quotation marks around a line or phrase that you plan to quote. Then have them rewrite a different paragraph using those techniques. Nancie Atwell edited a book called *Coming to Know: Writing to Learn in the Intermediate Grades* (Heinemann, 1990), which has excellent chapters on teaching students to be accurate note takers.

* Ask your librarian to show your students various types of reference materials on their topics, including videos, nonfiction magazines, informational picture books, and CD-ROMs. Stockpile a variety of references in your classroom as well.

* Let your students know ahead of time how many references you require. Teach them how to write a bibliography that follows the conventional form (alphabetical order, underlined title, publisher, and date).

* Have your students interview experts on the subject they are studying. Remind them to prepare their questions in advance.

* Show your class examples of high-quality reports and projects created by students in a previous year.

* Provide examples of nonfiction writing about history, social studies, and science for your students to read and discuss. *Ranger Rick*, *Cobblestone*, *Faces*, *Zillions*, *World*, and *Scholastic News* magazines are good resources for articles.

Create Your Own Rubrics

Whether you plan to assess your students' work for a study of Arctic animals, story analysis, or essay writing, creating your own rubrics is primarily a matter of defining for yourself the qualities of an exemplary student performance and then working from there to determine the characteristics of other performance levels. Here are some guideposts to get you started.

🌼 If you are assessing projects or reports that your students have already completed, collect the work products.

🌼 If you are assessing reading, select a text appropriate for your grade level that your students have not read—a good story with a theme appropriate for your grade level, a clear problem and resolution, and well-developed characters.

🌼 Design a prompt or project task that students can respond to in writing.

🌼 Along with sheets of lined paper on which they will write their final ideas, provide students with prewriting organizers such as webs, Venn diagrams, or lists of questions so students make notes about their ideas.

Create a Rubric

🌼 Look at the All-Purpose Rubrics on pages 121–127.

🌼 Notice that each level of the rubric provides the following: a number that represents the score; a developmental label; and a description of the product or performance. A four-level scale will allow you to make more precise assessments; however, at the beginning you may find a three-level rubric easier to use and sufficient for assessing most tasks or projects in your classroom.

Your next step is to determine the **key elements** of the performance or product you plan to assess. For example, if you are planning to assess your students' rainforest research projects, you would want to look at their bibliographies, research note cards, and their projects. The key elements, therefore, might include: (1) the number of books a student read; (2) the degree of accurate, relevant information included on their research note cards; (3) the accuracy of the information conveyed by the project; and (4) the quality and care a project reflects through colorful and detailed artwork.

To assess their written reports, you might focus on the following key elements: (1) accuracy of ideas; (2) development of information through the use of details, examples, and explanations; (3) organization of the information; and (4) conventions and mechanics of writing.

Next, keeping the key elements in mind, you should divide your students' work products into three piles. Trust your impressions. Because you're familiar with the subject matter, you'll know just what to look for in your students' work.

Now you're ready to customize your rubric. Begin by looking through your "best work" pile again to determine what excellence looks like. Keeping the key elements in mind, select the three or four most significant criteria that constitute an excellent performance. (Too many criteria will make your assessments more difficult in the beginning.) Write your criteria on the blank lines at the highest level of the rubric.

Examine the remaining piles of reports once again to decide on the criteria that distinguish the middle and lower levels of your students' papers. Then list these criteria on the blank lines of the rubric. At this point, it's a good idea to involve your students in the process. Show them your rubric to be sure it makes sense to them. Encourage them to ask questions that will help you clarify the criteria.

SOME WORDS OF ADVICE

Don't expect your rubrics to be perfect. You can improve them after you have used them with your students. Continue to revise until a rubric works for you.

Invite a grade-level colleague to join you in rubric assessments. It always helps to have someone with whom you can discuss your ratings.

Help Your Students Use Peer- and Self-Assessments

There are four excellent ways to involve your students in the assessment process—through self-assessment checklists, through cooperative rubric planning, through assessment anchor papers, and through goal-setting. You will find that for most students, each of these strategies will contribute to learning and improvement in their work.

SELF-ASSESSMENT CHECKLISTS

- Develop self-assessment checklists to match the rubrics you create. You may want to refer to the checklists in this book to help you do this.

- Model the process of self-assessment using a checklist. You can easily demonstrate it by thinking aloud as you critique your own performance or work product.

- Have students work with a partner to peer-assess each other's work. They can use a checklist to guide them.

COOPERATIVE RUBRIC PLANNING AND ASSESSMENT ANCHOR PAPERS

Once your students have become familiar with rubric assessments, they can play a greater role in the development process. Here's a good way to help them create their own rubrics:

- Make copies of the exemplary writing samples in this book (one for each of the students). If you have an overhead projector, you can make transparencies to show on an overhead screen.

- Have your students work with a partner to list three or four criteria that make each sample so good.

- List their observations on a chart or chalkboard beneath the heading "Criteria for an Excellent Essay" (or whatever writing genre is being assessed). Be sure to add your own ideas to your students' suggestions.

- Distribute copies of a writing rubric to each pair of students. Point out how labels (*strong, satisfactory, needs improvement*) or numbers (4, 3, 2, 1) are used to identify various performance levels.

- Next, have students fold a blank sheet of paper lengthwise into three boxes. They can also use a ruler for drawing lines to separate the boxes if they wish.

- Have them write the number 3 in the upper box, a 2 in the middle box, a 1 in the lower box.

- Tell your students to begin their rubric by copying the criteria they developed for an excellent essay in the first box. Then tell them to think of criteria to describe a satisfactory essay and write their ideas in the middle box. Finally have them think about what a not-so-good essay might look like and write those descriptions in the lowest box.

You'll find that your students' level of concern for the work they produce is even higher when they use a rubric they have cooperatively designed. Just as rubric creation focuses a teacher's instructional planning on the key elements to be learned and demonstrated, so does this process heighten students' awareness of what a successful piece of work demands.

GOAL SETTING

Once your students understand the criteria for a project, paper, or performance, they will be ready to establish their learning goals. To make this process easier, have your students examine a work product or a record form such as a book list. Then tell them to think about how they might improve their work and write their ideas on the goal-setting form on page 113.

Following are samples of fourth graders' goal-setting work.

Sample Goal-Setting Sheets

Name **Eric S.**   Date **Jan. 18**

Goal Setting

Description of work/project: My Reading Record Book List

What I notice: I've been reading more and harder books since September. I don't read Franklin Dixon's Hardy Boys as much now. I read books by different authors. The Last Laugh and Whipping Boy took a while to read.

My goal: to try to read harder books—funny books, biographies, information books, maybe short stories.

Name **Sarah D.**   Date **May 10**

Goal Setting

Description of work/project: My Reading Notebook Entries

What I notice: This entry shows that I can find a character's feelings and find out why they feel that way by something that happened in the book. I wrote that Robin didn't like living with her dad because her father thought that girls can't do anything and I gave an example.

My goal: to get to the exciting part sooner. Do you have a technique for reading fast?

Name _____ Date _____

Goal Setting

Description of work/project: _____

_____

What I notice: _____

_____

_____

_____

_____

My goal: _____

_____

- -

Name _____ Date _____

Goal Setting

Description of work/project: _____

_____

What I notice: _____

_____

_____

_____

_____

My goal: _____

_____

Closing Thoughts

Reflections on Rubric Assessment

Just when we think we have learned all we need to know about teaching and assessing reading and writing, something new comes along that turns each of us into learners again. I believe that the time we spend learning about rubrics, however, will be worthwhile. For example, if you've already experimented with a few of the rubrics in this book, you may have found several useful tools for assessing complex reading and writing activities and projects. And, if you've also included your students in the rubric assessment process, then you've probably discovered another equally important benefit. Once students understand the criteria by which their work will be judged, they are likely to create something better than they have ever produced before.

Lorrie LaCroix and Karen Maine—two teachers in Cubberly School in Long Beach, California—made this discovery when they asked students who had been using rubrics from fourth through seventh grade to write their responses to the question: "Do you think rubrics help you improve your work? Why or why not?" Some examples of student responses follow.

🌸 "I think rubrics really help me improve my work because since I've been using them, I've been getting good grades..."

🌸 "Rubrics help you improve your work because you are told right away what is expected of you."

🌸 "Whether I use it on my paper or someone else does it, it gives me a chance to see how I can improve."

🌸 "I like the way they word the scores and also how they show you how to get that score..."

🌸 "...they help make things fair so a student can't complain about his grade, and it also gives the teacher backup for a grade she made."

The students' responses also advise us to use rubrics judiciously by not overusing them, making them too complex, or relying solely upon them for determining a student's grade.

❂ "The worst thing is that if you're off by just a little bit from the rubric, your score goes down."

❂ "I'm getting tired of rubrics because we even have a rubric at lunch which is ridiculous."

❂ "They're not always easy to understand."

SUMMING UP: WHAT WE'VE LEARNED ABOUT RUBRICS

As the newest arrivals on the assessment scene, rubrics offer several important advantages to a balanced assessment program. Rubrics allow us to make meaningful evaluations of our students' reading comprehension and writing abilities. They also improve the traditional use of letter or numerical grading because they allow us to coach, rather than simply judge, our students' work. A rubric's explanations show students just what they need to do to produce a high-level paper or project. Rubrics also make it easier for students to assess their own work and set goals for future projects and performances. You will find blank forms for creating your own rubrics on pages 121–128 . It's a good idea to develop a matching self-assessment form for your students too. After experimenting with your new tools, make changes that will improve them. Then share your rubrics with other teachers, parents, and your principal so that you can work together on integrating authentic assessments with your district's grading and testing requirements. I wish you much success as you engage in the evolving and exciting process of rubric assessment.

Adele Fiderer

Appendix

A Sampling of Teacher's Rubrics Across the Curriculum

◀ EXAMPLE 1

Scoring Guide for Book Response Papers

Elements	**4**	**3**	**2**	**1**
Book choice	challenging	appropriate	acceptable	unacceptable
Format was followed	completely	mostly	to some degree	barely, if at all
Topic development	fully done with concrete details	mostly done with adequate details	details are adequate, but could be developed further	minimal development, vague, few details
Editing	almost no editing mistakes	a few mistakes and little interference with meaning	some mistakes, but they don't affect meaning much	several errors; meaning is affected

Rubric by Shelley Jackson, grades 6, 7, 8, The Brooklin School, Brooklin, Maine

EXAMPLE 2 ▶

Self-Assessment Form for Book Response Writing

Name_____ Date _____

	Yes	Somewhat	No
1. I selected a challenging book.	☐	☐	☐
2. My writing followed the format.	☐	☐	☐
3. I fully developed my writing and used concrete details.	☐	☐	☐
4. I corrected my spellings, punctuations, and paragraphs.	☐	☐	☐

Reading Project Scoring Guide

Book Summary Project
(Choice of poster, oral presentation, book report, or reading journal)

3 = Content

The project/ demonstrates superior understanding of the plot. The finished presentation is fully developed and well-organized.

Appearance/Editing
The final form of the project is neatly presented with few or no errors (spelling, punctuation, paragraphs).

2 = Content

The project/writing demonstrates moderate understanding of the plot. Some details may be lacking, but the project/writing is adequately developed and organized.

Appearance/Editing
The final form of the project is acceptably presented with some errors (spelling, punctuation, paragraphs)

1 = Content

It is difficult to understand the plot. The project/writing is minimally developed and may be disorganized.

Appearance/Editing
May be sloppy, with many editing errors.

◀ EXAMPLE 3

Developed by Shelley Jackson, grades 6,7,8, The Brooklin School, Brooklin, Maine

EXAMPLE 4 ▶

Developed by Suzanne Kaback, grade 5, The Holbrook School, Holden, Maine

Reading Project: Essay: Connecting a Book to Its Genre

Description of the task:
Read a book in one of the following genres: mystery, historical fiction, realistic fiction, autobiography, or fantasy. Write a three-paragraph essay to explain why the book is an example of that particular genre.

Goals of the task:
- to use details that connect the book to its genre
- to write an essay with a clear introduction, body, and conclusion
- to edit and neatly recopy the writing

LEVEL 3

Content
The essay clearly proves why the book is an example of a particular genre. Elements of the genre are given, and many details from the book are used to demonstrate why the book belongs to the genre. The essay has a clear introduction, body, and conclusion.

Appearance/Editing
The essay is neatly written and shows few or no errors.

LEVEL 2

Content
The essay lacks some details about the genre or about the book. It may not have a clear introduction, body, or conclusion.

Appearance/Editing
The essay has been rewritten and shows some editing errors.

LEVEL 1

Content
Many important details are missing. An introduction, body, or conclusion is missing.

Appearance/Editing
The essay shows many errors and/or is sloppy.

Scoring Guide for Assessing ___ Book Reports

Description of the task:

Read a challenging novel that you can understand.
Write a three-paragraph paper using concrete details and examples to explain your ideas about the story. In the first paragraph describe the plot of the story. In the second paragraph describe the main character. In the third paragraph give your opinion of the book. Be sure to edit your paper and recopy it.

Key Elements	4	3	2	1
Content	challenging	appropriate	acceptable	unacceptable
Format was followed	completely	mostly	to some degree	barely, if at all
Topic development	fully done with concrete details	mostly done with adequate details	details are adequate, but could be developed further	minimal development, vague, few details
Editing	almost no editing mistakes	a few mistakes and little interference with meaning	some mistakes, but they don't affect meaning much	several errors; meaning is affected

EXAMPLE 5

Developed by Shelley Jackson, grades 6,7,8, The Brooklin School, Brooklin, Maine

See page 121 for a reproducible adaptation of this rubric.

EXAMPLE 6 ▶

Developed by Carol DeMay and Frances Seaman, grade 3, Guardino Elementary School, Thousand Island School District, New York

Silent Reading Rubric

Proficient:

- ◉ Has book ready to read
- ◉ Uses reading time wisely
- ◉ Selects books on his/her level (can retell main events)
- ◉ Chooses to read a variety of genres
- ◉ Reading log always:
    - is dated correctly
    - lists book titles and genre, gives last page read, indicates if book was completed or put back (discontinued)
    - is neat and legible

Capable:

- ◉ Generally has book ready to read
- ◉ Usually uses reading time wisely
- ◉ Usually selects books on his/her level
- ◉ Chooses some variety of genre
- ◉ Reading log generally:
    - is dated correctly
    - lists book titles and genre, gives last page read, indicates if book was completed or put back (discontinued)
    - is neat and legible

Incomplete:

- ◉ Seldom has book ready to read
- ◉ Uses reading time inappropriately
- ◉ Has difficulty choosing books at his/her level
- ◉ Reads little variety of genre
- ◉ Reading log:
    - inconsistently shows dates, book titles, pages read, and completions
    - is illegible and/or disorganized

Grade Level Reading Performance
Grade 4   Reading Levels

Minimum   Articles in magazines and newspapers such as:
Ranger Rick, Scienceland, Zoo News

Fiction such as:
Stuart Little   (White)
Fantastic Mr. Fox   (Dahl)
Ramona Quimby, age 8 (Cleary)
or Runaway Ralph   (Cleary) or Ribsy by Cleary
Abel's Island   (Steig)

Typical   Articles in magazines and newspapers such as:
Cricket, Contact Kids, Sports Illustrated for Kids, Time for Kids

Fiction such as:
Anastasia Krupnik   (Lowry)
Wayside School is Falling Down (Sachar)
Super Fudge   (Blume)
Charlotte's Web   (White)
The Pinballs   (Byars)

Advanced   Articles in magazines and newspapers such as:
National Geographic World, sports section of newspapers, American Girl

Fiction such as:
Number the Stars   (Lowry)
Call It Courage   (Sperry)
The Great Gilly Hopkins (Paterson)
The Summer of the Swans (Byars)

▲

*Adapted from a rubric developed by teachers in
Scarsdale Public Schools, New York. See
page 127 for a blank form of this rubric.*

Blank Forms
for Customized
Rubric Design

Scoring Guide for Assessing _____

Description of the task: _____

Levels of Achievement

For each key element, describe various degrees of achievement in meeting the task's goals.

Key Elements	**4** strong	**3** appropriate	**2** acceptable	**1** unacceptable
Content				
Directions Followed	completely	mostly	to some degree	barely
Development of Ideas				
Editing				

All-Purpose Rubric for Assessing _____

task

Description of the task's goals:

_____

_____

_____

Scores

3 **Proficient**

The work product or performance achieves all goals set for the task. It is complete and indicates a very good understanding of the knowledge required to complete the task.

_____

_____

2 **Satisfactory**

The work product or performance achieves many of the goals set for task. It is almost complete and indicates an adequate understanding of the knowledge required to complete the task.

_____

_____

1 **Developing**

The work product or performance achieves some of the goals set for the task. It is partially complete and indicates a limited understanding of the knowledge required to complete the task.

_____

_____

0 **Novice**

The product or response does not meet the basic requirements of the task. Although there may be an attempt to meet one or two of the task's requirements, the response is incomplete.

_____

_____

40 Rubrics & Checklists to Assess Reading and Writing   Scholastic Professional Books

Rubric for Assessing

_____

(name of student's project or performance)

Key elements of the project or performance:

_____

Use the blank lines to describe specific aspects of student's work at each level.

3 **Capable (Criteria for a successful project or performance):**

_____

_____

_____

_____

2 **Satisfactory**

_____

_____

_____

_____

1 **Beginning**

_____

_____

_____

_____

Rubric for Individual Assessments

Student's Name _____ Date _____

Performance/Product _____ Score _____

Key Elements of the task:

_____ _____ _____ _____

Use the blank lines below to describe the quality of a student's work for each of the key elements.

3 **Strong** _____

_____

_____

_____

2 **Satisfactory** _____

_____

_____

_____

1 **Needs Some Improvement** _____

_____

_____

_____

0 **Needs Much Improvement** _____

_____

_____

_____

40 Rubrics & Checklists to Assess Reading and Writing   Scholastic Professional Books

Rubric for Writing, Projects, and Performances

Key Elements of an Excellent _____

(name of the specific writing topic, project, or performance)

Description of key elements:

_____

_____

_____

_____

_____

_____

Scoring Guide

4   All key elements are well developed.

3   Some key elements are well developed.
Others are adequately developed.

2   Some key elements are adequately developed. Others are not.

1   No key elements are adequately developed.

Name _____

Reading Comprehension Score _____

Rubric for Assessing
Report Card Writing (Individual)

Subject/Topic: _____

Comprehension of Subject/Topic:	Level **3**	Level **2**	Level **1**
Writing Effectiveness:			
Idea Development			
Organization			
Language Usage			
Mechanics			

Grade Level Reading Performance
Grade _____ Reading Levels

Minimum	Articles in magazines and newspapers such as: _____ _____ Fiction such as: _____ _____ _____ _____ _____
Typical	Articles in magazines and newspapers such as: _____ _____ Fiction such as: _____ _____ _____ _____ _____
Advanced	Articles in magazines and newspapers such as: _____ _____ Fiction such as: _____ _____ _____ _____

40 Rubrics & Checklists to Assess Reading and Writing   Scholastic Professional Books

Class Record Form

Names of Students

40 Rubrics & Checklists to Assess Reading and Writing   Scholastic Professional Books